A Penny's Worth
of Minced Ham

Another Look at the Great Depression

Robert J. Hastings

Southern Illinois University Press
CARBONDALE AND EDWARDSVILLE

Edited by Margaret Sattler
Production supervised by Natalia Nadraga
89 88 87 86   4 3 2 1

Library of Congress Cataloging-in-Publication Data
Hastings, Robert J.
   A penny's worth of minced ham.

   (Shawnee books)
   1. Hastings, Robert J.—Childhood and youth.
2. Marion (Ill.)—Biography   3. Depressions—1929—
United States—Personal narratives.   4. United States—
Social life and customs—1918–1945.   I. Title.
II. Series.
F549.M34H374   1986   977.3′993   [B]   85-31731
ISBN 0-8093-1303-0
ISBN 0-8093-1304-9 (pbk.)

To my wife, Bessie Emling Hastings, with whom I celebrated our fortieth anniversary the year I wrote this book

You bet I remember those neighborhood stores where you'd buy a "poke of sugar" or "a poke of coffee." Some mornings, on my way to catch my ride to the mines, if we'd slept late, I'd stop in a little store for a pastry, or maybe something for my dinner bucket . . . and then the Depression closed the mines and there was no bucket to buy food for. I walked my legs off looking for work all over Williamson and Franklin counties. It got to where a mine manager would see me coming and start shaking his head. I knew, and he knew, what he meant.

—Landon Henderson, retired coal miner,
Marion, Illinois

Contents

ix . . . *Illustrations*
xi . . . *Preface*

1 . . . A Trip to Swan's Store
9 . . . To Lon Norman's for Ice
18 . . . The Short Way to Kroger's
24 . . . The Long Way to Kroger's
29 . . . A Sack of Bread at Bertha's
41 . . . An Unbroken Thread
46 . . . Two Loaves of Twin Bread
54 . . . A Trip to West Frankfort
67 . . . Brilliantine, Coal Buckets, and Tootsie Rolls
76 . . . The Street Merchant Go-Getters
80 . . . What! Shop with a Baby Buggy?
86 . . . Relish the Moment
91 . . . Good Night, Sweet Prince

97 . . . *Epilogue*
99 . . . *Appendix: Grocery Stores in Marion, Illinois, 1939*

Illustrations

xvi . . . Hastings family reunion, 1912

(*following page 29*)

Robert J. Hastings, 1924
Robert J. Hastings, 1927
Robert J. Hastings, 1928
Eldon Hastings, 1930s
Ruby Hastings, 1930s
Eldon Hastings, 1949
Eldon and Ruby Hastings, 1956
Hastings family home, 1959

(*following page 55*)

Matthews General Store, Pinckneyville, about 1918
Interior of A. C. Elliott's Grocery, Johnston City, 1920s
Interior of W. R. Hodge General Merchandise,
Marion, 1927
Interior of Leming's Butcher Shop and Grocery,
West Frankfort, 1920s
Interior of Kroger's, Pinckneyville, late 1920s or
early 1930s

Interior of Holmes Grocery and Meat Market,
Marion, 1920s
Interior of Everett Fitzgerald's Grocery,
West Frankfort, 1937
Interior of grocery at St. Libory, about 1970
Stout's General Merchandise, Gale, about 1970
Clover Farm Store, Marissa, 1985

Preface

IN THE HEART of that triangle of Illinois known as Little Egypt is my hometown of Marion. I was born there on May 17, 1924, in the front bedroom of my parents' home at 1404 North State Street. I was the youngest of four children, all delivered by the family doctor, J. G. Parmley.

In September of 1929, Mom decided I was old enough to start school—although the rules said you had to be six by January 1, and I wouldn't be six until the following May. "Sometimes Mr. Belford allows five-year-olds in the first grade if they behave," she told me. "You can go for one day and see what happens. Nothing's to be lost by trying."

Since Mr. H. O. Belford was the city superintendent of schools and a member of the First Baptist Church, whatever Mr. Belford said was the gospel. Mom had admired him from the time they were in the same eighth grade class at the old Washington School.

"Mr. Belford went on to college and made something of himself," she frequently commented. "He was big for his age and the other boys made fun because he could barely squeeze into his desk seat. But he paid no mind and got his education."

Since Mom had completed only the eighth grade, she stood almost in awe at Mr. Belford's judgment as to when a youngster was ready for school. She often made me sad when she added, "I could have been somebody, too, made something of myself, if I'd stayed in school."

I never doubted that Mom was "somebody," regardless of her formal training. What she meant was a career of her own. No doubt she would have succeeded, since she was a self-starter, well-organized, a fast reader, and liked people. But when she dropped out of school in 1907, a girl's place was in the home, with a few exceptions here and there for schoolteachers, telephone operators, stenographers, and nurses.

Anyway, I marched off to the Jefferson School on East Boulevard with her words embedded in my mind, "If Mr. Belford says so, you can stay."

The teacher had barely assigned our seats and taken our names when I grew restless. I knew I didn't have to stay—according to the law! And I didn't want to. I was the youngest and smallest. I felt out of place. So taking destiny in my own hands, I got up and calmly walked out the door, down the steps, then broke into a run down Boulevard toward home. I was a runaway!

Grace MacDonald, our teacher, sent an older boy after me, but I outran him. I looked back only once. I can see him still, calling to me with his hands cupped to his mouth, "Come back . . . come back . . . the teacher said to come back."

When I got home I told Mom, "I don't like it. I'm not going to that old school and I never will!" She quietly told me to change into my play clothes and commented, "Mr. Belford probably wouldn't have let you stay, anyway."

Seven weeks later was Black Tuesday—October 24, 1929, that infamous day when the stock market crashed on Wall Street in New York City. My goodness—was I the cause of that? Had I sat quietly at my little desk in the Jefferson School—my place of duty—would this calamity have befallen our country?

Admittedly, such a thought never entered my mind. New York City was too far from Marion for that. But Marion was not too far to feel the fury of the Great Depression, the worst economic debacle in the history of the United States. For more than ten years it held its grip on our nation, especially on southern Illinois.

By the end of 1929, investors had lost $40 billion on the stock market. Before the Depression ended, 5,000 banks failed and 32,000 businesses went bankrupt. Despairing men sold apples on street corners, ate in soup kitchens, and lived in clumps of shacks called "Hoovervilles," after President Herbert Hoover. In Chicago, fifty men were seen fighting over a single barrel of garbage in the alley back of a restaurant.

Marion is in Williamson County, which along with Saline and Franklin counties was identified by the federal government as one of fifty distinct depressed areas in the nation. All told, thirty-four banks in those three counties failed. Merchants paid their bills with post office money orders. Teachers were paid in warrants, for which they were lucky to get fifty cents on the dollar. The town of Benton, just north of Marion, got so low on funds it had to turn off the street lights.

My earlier book, *A Nickel's Worth of Skim Milk*, describes those grim thirties as seen through the eyes of a grade-school boy. Published in 1972 by University Publications at Southern Illinois University, this book enjoyed a wide readership and won two awards. Hundreds of readers wrote thanking me. Many of them added, "It was really my story, too, for I had the same experiences."

I guess one proof of a helpful book is whether it's a mirror in which we see ourselves. About 1975, I was speaking at McKendree College in Lebanon, Illinois. An elderly woman, using a walker, came to hear me. "What in the world is an old, broken-down widow like me doing here?" she asked with a twinkling smile, after straining up the steps.

"I'll tell you why," she continued. "A year ago I broke my hip, then had to sell my lovely home and move into government subsidized housing. I didn't like it. I didn't like the neighbors, the tiny rooms, the change in lifestyle. Hospitalized, I stopped eating, grew weaker, talked to no one. Then someone gave me your 'Skim Milk' book. It recalled my own youth and the struggles of my parents. I remembered how they had triumphed in spite of hardships.

"I started crying . . . and then I broke out laughing . . . and then I cried some more. A nurse, upset, called my doctor, saying I was out of my head. He told her not to worry, that this was a sign I was breaking out of my depression. I vowed then to get up out of that bed and make the best of what I have left. And I did— and that's why I'm here to meet the author who showed me myself."

A number of friends have encouraged me to write a sequel. Until now I've hesitated, aware that the success of one book doesn't guarantee the popularity of another. But now, sixteen years later, I've decided to revisit Marion in the thirties. This time I'm writing about the neighborhood grocery stores of that era. Again, the Great Depression will be the backdrop for most of the book.

Whether or not you lived through the Depression, you probably have nostalgic memories of a neighborhood store some-where that you went for candy and soda and where your parents bought their groceries.

Now how do you get to Marion? Well, let's see. It's on Inter-state 57, just sixty miles north of Cairo, where the marriage of the Mississippi and Ohio rivers takes place. Marion is in that arrow-like, wedge-shaped tip of Illinois, forty miles to the west of the Ohio River and forty miles to the east of the Mississippi. It's in the land between the rivers. It's also in the land between yesterday and tomorrow, which means anyone can find it!

Oh, one other thing. You will often see the phrase, "As I re-member." That's because I've tried to base the book on how I saw things as a boy. I may be in error here and there. But this is how I remember it.

A Penny's Worth of Minced Ham

Hastings family reunion at 1404 North State Street, Marion, Illinois, about 1912. Seated in front are John Hise and Edie Grove Hastings, the author's grandparents. The author's mother, Ruby, is second from left. The author's father, Eldon, second from left in the back row, is holding the author's sister, Afton Margaret.

A TRIP TO THE SWAN'S STORE

Bobby, take this quarter and run down to Mr. Swan's store. Ask for fifteen cents worth of minced ham and a dime loaf of bread. When you get home, I'll fry the minced ham and make us some milk gravy for supper.

Those were Mom's instructions on an afternoon in late July 1933.

I was nine years old at the time, enjoying summer vacation between the third and fourth grades. We lived in a five-room house at 1404 North State Street in Marion, where my parents had moved in 1914. My paternal grandparents had lived there when it was just a four-room house, later enclosing a porch for a fifth room.

The warmest and tenderest memories of my childhood are embedded in that house. When my parents sold it in 1957, having lived there forty-three years, I cried uncontrollably when I got off by myself.

The best way to describe the house is to say that it was typical of the thirties—two bedrooms, kitchen, dining or sitting room with a heating stove, and living room. What we didn't have makes a long list: no clothes closets (except a walk-in pantry), no bathroom, no kitchen sink, no hot water heater, no microwave oven or toaster, no television, no telephone, no central heating, no air conditioning, no storm windows or insulation, no refrigerator or freezer, no disposal or blender, no washing machine, and no electrical outlets except a bare bulb dangling at the end of a black cord in the center of each room (which means you groped around in the dark until you finally found the little button that switched on the light).

Like thousands of miners in southern Illinois, Dad lost his job when the Great Depression forced so many of the mines to shut down. We survived the Depression for two reasons: First, Dad's willingness to take any and every odd job. And second, Mom's ability to stretch every penny to its maximum potential.

My boyhood diary shows that Dad sold iron cords from door to door, "worked a day in the hay," bought a horse to break gardens (a disaster!), rented an extra lot for a garden to be planted on the shares, picked peaches, raised and sold sweet potatoes slips, traded an occasional dozen of eggs at the grocery, and hung wallpaper.

He also "painted Don Albright's house for $5," picked up a day's work now and then at the Spillertown strip mines, guarded the fence during the Williamson County Fair, cut hair for boys in the neighborhood, and sold coal orders. When he had to and could, he worked intermittently on WPA (a government make-work program) or picked up an occasional "relief" (welfare) order of powdered milk, grapefruit, beans, meal, and flour.

Money being scarce, we learned to save back until we had the exact amount for a purchase. This explains why Mom asked me to get fifteen cents worth of lunch meat—rather than a half pound or so—since we might not know exactly how much that would cost. But fifteen cents worth of navy beans, a dime loaf of bread, or twenty cents worth of bananas meant exactly what you said!

I jumped at the chance to run the errand to Swan's Store, located for many years at 105 East DeYoung Street.

For one thing, I liked Mom's milk gravy as much as Esau in Old Testament days enjoyed Jacob's red pottage.

As a boy, I cared little for peas, green beans, spinach, and the like. But I devoured cream-style corn, mashed potatoes, cole slaw, and milk gravy. Mom could make milk gravy from the drippings of nearly anything—sausage, bacon, pork chops, fried chicken, hamburger meat, or even lunch meat such as bologna or minced ham. In fact, she kept a special jar on the back of the stove for drippings so that if we were out of meat, she still could make a "dab of gravy."

Milk gravy's easy to make. You start with a hot skillet of drippings into which you sprinkle flour and a pinch of salt, stirring constantly until there is a smooth mixture of fat and flour. There's no excuse for lumpy gravy so long as you are patient to stir it enough, preferably with a fork so you can mash the lumps. Next you add milk or cream, again stirring constantly so it won't stick to the pan. Bring it to a boil and let it bubble until it thickens. If too thick, you can always add more milk. If too thin, add more flour. Forget a recipe—use your own judgment.

Milk gravy is best over hot biscuits, fresh from the oven. Mom insisted we be at the table a minute or two before the biscuits were brown. In her mind, biscuits were hot only if they were so warm to her touch that she had to use a dishcloth to pass them. Steaming, that is. Then the almost boiling gravy on top of the steaming biscuits. Careful—don't burn your tongue.

Another delicacy with milk gravy was steamed bread, made with dry or leftover bakery bread. Mom used an aluminum club steamer to boil the water, topped with a perforated rack on which the bread rested, then covered with a tight lid. The steam moistened the stale bread until it was hot and fresh-tasting. A delicacy of the Depression if I ever tasted one!

Mom also made what she called "thickening gravy" prepared with flour and beef drippings, say, from a roast. Red-eye gravy came from the drippings of country ham, which forms an "eye" in the skillet. But since this gravy was rare at our house, I don't know how to make it.

Once or twice during the worst part of the Depression I remember Mom making water gravy. With no milk in the house she would take, say, bacon drippings, stir in flour and salt, then add water. She and Dad ate it, but I couldn't stomach it as the taste was flat and insipid. Fortunately, I was never forced to eat what I didn't like. I think that's one reason I enjoy nearly any kind of food today (except boiled okra!).

But back to my shopping trip to Swan's. With a final reminder not to lose that quarter, which by now was wrapped securely in a handkerchief in a pocket of my bib overalls, I cut across the back alley to North Glendale, then down to East DeYoung and the store.

It was a typical, one-room neighborhood grocery of the thirties. A shed roof extended across the front porch where, in the summer, watermelons, apples, peaches, fresh corn, and the like were displayed. A long metal sign above the porch identified it as a "Clover Farm Store." In the thirties, you could pick up little story leaflets with your groceries that included puzzles, jokes, and Clover Farm ads. Two big plate glass windows were on either side of the front door, to which was affixed a tinkling bell to alert Mr. Swan and his helper, Webb Eason, that they had a customer.

To the left, as you entered, Mr. Swan displayed dry goods such as bolts of calico, gingham, unbleached muslin, or patterned dress material. You could also buy needles, pins, sewing thread, elastic, lace, ribbons, buttons, thimbles, dress patterns, work gloves, handkerchiefs, and the like.

On the right was a coal heating stove, plus shelves for canned goods and open boxes of bulk cookies. A big stalk of bananas hung from a hook in the ceiling. In the spring, Mr. Swan assembled kites and fastened them to the walls. Some of the kites had pictures on the paper—Niagara Falls, dirigibles, the Washington Monument, and the like.

At the rear was a short, squat meat display case. Back then, nothing was prepackaged in neat plastic trays. If you could afford a roast, some pork chops, or a steak, Mr. Swan would take the larger piece of meat from the case, lay it on his butcher block, reach overhead for his cleaver and knives, and cut exactly what you ordered.

So when I ordered my fifteen cents worth of minced ham, Mr. Swan reached inside the case for a long roll, then sliced off what he thought would come to that amount. Once he weighed the slices, he tore off a piece of butcher paper from a roll mounted at the end of the counter—complete with its own cutter—and wrapped the meat. Finally he reached overhead for the string that unraveled from a cone-shaped ball and tied and knotted the package.

"Now son," he said, "with your dime loaf of bread and counting the penny sales tax, that will be a total of twenty-six cents."

My heart sank. I didn't have the extra penny! Illinois had just levied a sales tax the first of that month—July 1, 1933. Folks just weren't accustomed to it. In fact, some of our neighbors vowed they'd never pay that tax. They did, of course, but many felt it was unfair to levy a new tax, especially on food, right at the worst of the Depression.

When I confessed I had only a quarter, Mr. Swan turned a little red in the face, then said, "You kids must learn to bring that sales tax. I have to pay it and you're going to pay it. Here, I'm going to teach you a lesson."

Having no earthly idea what kind of a lesson he was about to teach an innocent nine-year-old Depression kid in overalls, I waited for judgment to fall. Mr. Swan proceeded to untie the package, reach for his butcher knife, and slice off a tiny sliver which he pitched back in the refrigerator. (Imagine how tiny it would be at today's prices—it would probably require a microscope to find it!)

I now had a dime loaf of bread, fourteen cents worth of lunch meat, and one cent for the Illinois sales tax, totaling exactly a quarter. And Mr. Swan had his penny's worth of minced ham.

I'll not reveal what my mother said when I got home, but it would make interesting reading. However, we didn't let that spoil our supper of fried lunch meat, milk gravy, and steamed bread.

A few days later, at dusk, I was playing in the front yard. Out of the corner of my eye I spotted a new DeSoto inching its way along East Patrick Street; it then turned on to North State and passed our house. Sitting proudly in the front seat were Mr. and Mrs. Swan. They were a short couple and I can still see Mr. Swan straining to see over the dashboard. I wondered then how his feet could reach the clutch and brakes.

The DeSoto automobile, no longer manufactured, was a classy car in its day. I was really impressed, for I never remember seeing *anyone* drive a brand-spanking new car. Oh, I'd seen new cars on display in the big showrooms of the Davis Brothers Motor Company at 700 North Market. But I never dreamed anyone actually bought them. I thought they were to look at.

Who in the world could find $780 or so to buy a new DeSoto in 1933? My boyish mind came up with the answer: Mr. Swan could, because he knew how to slice the ham thin!

Dad explained that when you buy a new car, you must drive it slowly for several miles to break it in properly. I said to myself, "When I get big and buy a new car, the first thing I'll do is drive real slow around the neighborhood, right after supper while everyone's outside playing or sitting in lawn chairs, so all my friends can see me."

Unfortunately, by the time I bought a new car that I felt was a match for Mr. Swan's (a 1962 Oldsmobile I purchased in Louisville, Kentucky), the rules had changed. "Take it out on the highway and drive the devil out of it the first few hundred miles," the salesman told me. My boyhood dream faded, and great was the fading thereof!

The Dodge and DeSoto dealer in Marion at the time was the Swan Motor Company at 309 West Main. Was this a relative? Is this why Mr. Swan picked a DeSoto? I don't know. But I've long since forgiven Mr. Swan. After all, he had to pay the tax so why shouldn't I—even at the expense of seeing a sliver of my supper thrown back in the meat case?

I've often wondered if anyone had a similar experience. Glenn Travelstead, a long-time neighbor at 1406 North State, tells me he did.

"I know what you mean by saving up until you had the exact amount during the Depression," Glenn told me. "About the time the sales tax was passed, I had put back exactly $1.98 to buy a new pair of Osh Kosh B'Gosh overalls for Glenn, Jr. I picked out a pair at Powell's Best Clothes in Egypt, located at 205 Public Square. Mr. Kelton, the clerk, wrapped them for me, then said that would be $2.02 including tax. For the life of me, I didn't have the extra four cents.

"So Mr. Kelton put the overalls back on the shelf and I went home to find four pennies. At the time, I was doing odd jobs for Alice Wallace, a neighbor, such as washing woodwork, mowing the lawn, and milking her goats, for which she paid me twenty cents an hour. Mrs. Wallace kindly advanced me enough for the sales tax and the next day I went downtown to pick up the overalls."

In a similar vein—although it's not related to the sales tax—Ed Handkins remembers when he got less than he went for. Ed, who grew up in Crab Orchard east of Marion, recalls going to a crossroads store at the little community of Corinth when he was about four years old.

"Each time I went with my parents to buy groceries, I would get a double-dip ice-cream cone for a nickel," he told me. "Then one day, without warning and as an economy move, the storekeeper gave me only one dip. I was so young that I took it personal—thought he maybe didn't like me anymore. So I called him a tight-wad, probably to his face."

Ed recalls another incident at Smith's Grocery in Crab Orchard when he was five years old. It wasn't painful to him, but it embarrassed his mom and dad no end. As Ed put it:

"We had killed hogs that day and someone took a pig's tail and fastened it to the seat of my pants with a safety pin. The tail was still there when we drove to the store in our pickup. I've never forgotten the kidding, just as I've never forgotten the missing dip of ice cream I thought I was entitled to."

The little stores with their quaint ways are a vanishing part of Americana. But to this day, I delight in handing a clerk the exact change, even though this means fumbling in my wallet and coin-holder. I notice most younger people put down a ten- or twenty-dollar bill, not bothering to fish around for the exact change. It's a habit with me, going back to when you bought exactly what you had money to pay for. Occasionally, I notice customers my age doing the same thing. Quite often the cashier will say, "Oh, you've got the exact change," as if that were some rare, undefinable coincidence.

We're a passing breed—at least in today's economy. But we're still ahead of those who never had to bother about counting every penny. You see, we got the fried minced ham and the milk gravy!

TO LON NORMAN'S FOR ICE

Bobby, take this nickel on the shelf and go down to Norman's Store and get us a chunk of ice. I'm making us some tea for dinner. Hurry now, dinner'll be on the table when you get home.

It was one of those dreadfully hot summers of 1936 or 1937 that produced the Dust Bowl out West, and the prospect of iced tea for dinner made me scamper.

Nothing glistened so brightly that summer as ice. In fact, the chunks we bought at Lon Norman's store sparkled like giant diamonds—treasures to use sparingly, to save back, to stretch as far as they would go.

Air conditioning was practically unknown in the thirties—and even had we known about it, we couldn't have afforded it. We were prisoners of the heat—yet our hot prisons made those iced drinks all the more appealing, as if it were almost worth it to be so hot so as to enjoy to the fullest something cold and icy.

Somehow we felt that if we could afford ice four or five days a week, our cold tea and lemonade would create magic oases that turned the brown grass to a lush green, the shimmering heat waves to spring breezes, and the white sheets on the clothesline to drifts of snow.

Oh, the drinking water we drew from a deep well was always moderately cool and refreshing. While working in the garden, Dad enjoyed drawing a "fresh bucket" and drinking it right there at the well curb. He'd hoist the whole bucket to his lips, letting some of the subterranean liquid spill down over his work clothes for the cooling effect, then throw out the rest.

Well water didn't stay cool very long when the temperature went past 100° day after day and Marionites with nothing else to do fried eggs on downtown sidewalks. That's why we always drew a "fresh bucket" when we needed a drink. But even our well water couldn't take the place of a glass of tea or lemonade made with chipped ice from Norman's Store.

There had been times, back in the twenties, when the iceman made regular deliveries to our door. On summer mornings, Mom would hang a square, black card with white lettering in the front window. Printed in white in the four corners were the numbers 25, 50, 75, and 100. If she wanted the iceman to bring, say, 50 pounds, she hung the card so that number was upright.

But the Depression jerked the ice card out of our window. I remember the little relic of an icebox from the twenties that stood on our back porch. During the thirties Mom used it to store canning jars and the like. A lid opened at the top so you could lower the ice into a compartment lined with galvanized zinc. Below, a door opened to reveal two or three small, shallow shelves. The whole thing would fit in the corner of some home refrigerators today.

When we had ice in the icebox, Mom kept a dishpan underneath to catch the water. Sometimes it ran over and formed puddles on the floor. "Oh, the ice pan's run over," Mom would say, while we grabbed rags to mop it up. We later solved this problem by drilling a hole in the kitchen floor, so the water could drip through a funnel under the house. No more messy pans.

Even then, before money was so scarce, Mom recycled the water from the ice pan by using it for hair-washing and the like. The reason was that this water was softer than our well water.

But all of that was past now, since we could afford ice

only in nickel chunks for cold drinks. For refrigeration, we put what little margarine and milk we had into a water bucket, then lowered it into the well where it kept moderately cool. One end of the rope was tied to a board that lay across the well curb. The rope was the right length so the bucket would just clear the water.

Some farm folks who had more milk would pour it into big glass jugs, then submerge them in the water, which kept the milk even colder. Woe be it if the jug came unplugged or two jugs banged against each other and broke, spilling the milk into the well and spoiling the drinking water.

I still haven't gotten to Norman's Store. First, let me tell you how I carried the ice home. Actually, I didn't carry it—I pulled it in a borrowed wagon. Here's why it was borrowed.

Being five years old when the Depression struck, I soon learned we couldn't afford everything. Some things I wanted I never even asked for. It wasn't that my parents scolded or snapped at me that we were poor. They never said we were poor. We refused to use that word. We'd talk about poor folks in general, as compared with those who had plenty, and we knew which category fitted us.

Mom and Dad didn't constantly remind me that "we can't afford this or that." It was a reality I sensed and accepted. Mine was an inner sense of what was appropriate to ask for, and not to ask for.

I recall some favorite, but inexpensive, toys. The first I remember is a little red firetruck that my sister, Afton, brought home from St. Louis. I must have been three or four. She let me play with it on Christmas Eve. I thought it was the shiniest, peppiest thing I'd ever seen.

At bedtime Dad said, "Now leave your new truck under the Christmas tree, and in the morning it will be there with the other toys that Santa brings."

"No!" I said. "Santa Claus will steal my new truck. I

don't want him to have it." I was adamant and insisted on "parking" it over in a corner, well out of sight. I guess I thought Santa would put it in his sack and give it to some less fortunate little boy.

I also had one of the smaller sets of Tinker Toys. I played with the knobs and sticks until they were worn and shrunken and no longer held together when I tried to build a ferris wheel. Mom soaked the pieces overnight in the washpan; the next morning it was as if I had a new set.

I grew up in the cowboy and Indian era and delighted in one or two inexpensive cap gun and holster sets. Then came that bright Christmas morning when I opened a package and found a real Indian outfit—brown cotton pants with fringes down both legs, a matching fringed shirt that hung loose over the belt, and a real honest-to-goodness headdress of dyed feathers.

For all I knew, it came direct from an Indian reservation in Arizona, even if it detoured through one of Sears' catalog offices. I played with a homemade bow and arrow, but somehow my arrows never went as straight or as far as they did in the Western movies.

Kids improvised many toys in the thirties. We assembled our own kites out of brown paper and paste made of flour and water. We played street hockey with sticks and crushed tin cans and rode on homemade scooters with wheels salvaged from old roller skates. When we played marbles, we made sure no one shot with a "steelie," which in the hands of a sharpshooter could shatter and ruin the glass marbles.

Mom used to time me as to how quickly I could assemble a puzzle of the forty-eight states of the Union. I got to where I could see the map of the United States in my sleep—big fat Texas; Florida and California with their long fingers reaching to the oceans; look-alikes North and South Dakota; thin Tennessee; Oklahoma with its index finger pointing to New Mexico; Montana and Wyoming "where the deer and the antelope play"; and tiny Vermont and New Hampshire.

And then came that wonder board game of the thirties—Monopoly! I played game after game, hour after hour, with my closest boyhood friend, Billy Roberts. We were mesmerized by the prospect of becoming overnight millionaires.

But leafing through the Sears and Montgomery-Ward catalogs, I found two prizes I dared not ask for. They cost too much. First was an all-purpose wagon with removable stakes. You could use it as a "farm" wagon to haul any and everything a kid might need to haul, or remove the stakes and "drive" it as a flatbed.

My second wish was for a tent. Camping was not all that big back then, and the tents I remember were designed for children's play in their own backyards. I can still see the catalog illustrations of the tents, with their extended awnings and poles, and children gaily playing. If I could go back and be a boy and own a wagon with real stakes and a tent with flaps that let down when it rained, I guess I'd take the Depression all over again in stride.

However, Glenn Travelstead, who lived next door and managed to save enough to buy his son Junior a pair of genuine Osh Kosh B'Gosh overalls, also saved enough to buy him an ordinary red wagon. So on special occasions—such as when I went for ice—I borrowed his.

Now you don't just haul off and go down to Norman's Store for ice without getting your equipment ready. After all, when the early settlers loaded their big, covered wagons for the long trek west to Oregon and California, they sometimes took weeks to pack.

The main supplies were old quilts, tow sacks, and maybe a tarpaulin to wrap the ice so it wouldn't melt. If Brink's armored cars take safeguards, why not make sure your ice gets home in one piece?

I often sat in our front porch swing and watched cars

pass with chunks of ice tilted on their rear bumpers. But watch how that exposed ice melts. You could see the drips right down the middle of the street. And by the time the driver got home, the ice had a big gash in one side where it had melted and settled onto the bumper. What a waste!

In the thirties, you saved everything—even the feathers from fryers who got their necks wrung in our backyard. What's cozier on a winter night than a feather bed or a pillow made with feathers? One relic we saved for years was an old piece of tarpaulin. I have no idea where it came from. I just know it was as much a part of our lives as getting up and going to bed. "Use that old tarp out in the smokehouse . . . Let's get that tarp in out of the rain . . . Help me roll it up . . . I wonder if that tarp is still any good . . . " Voices from the thirties, still echoing, still audible.

So on that morning in 1937, with a nickel in my pocket, I folded a tow sack, a worn homemade quilt, and the tarp into the bottom of Junior's wagon.

Pulling it behind me, I walked down State Street rather than taking a shortcut through the alley so I could be on a sidewalk all the way. Reaching DeYoung Street, I turned west and passed Mr. Swan's store, where I'd lost my penny's worth of minced ham.

A block further, at 100 East DeYoung, at the intersection of North Market and sitting astride a creek, was the Lon Norman store. At one time, Lon wanted Glenn Travelstead's place next door to us. He planned to tear down the house and put in a corner filling station. But they couldn't get together on a price so, fortunately, the neighborhood remained residential.

In front of Norman's Store was a small icehouse and two gas pumps. At that time you actually pumped the gasoline up into a glass cylinder on top. This was done by hand, using a leverlike handle. The gasoline squished

and frothed as it was pumped into the see-through glass
cylinder, which held ten gallons. When a customer wanted
gas, the fuel flowed by gravity into the tank. The cylinder
was calibrated with metal tabs indicating how many gallons had been bought.

Texaco Fire-Chief was highly advertised as a premium
gasoline. As I recall, Fire-Chief was a deeper red than
other brands, almost bloodlike in color. Whether it was
higher octane or artificial coloring, I don't know. In fact, I
didn't care, for I was more fascinated by the small, white,
thickly insulated ice house that stood nearby.

If you owned a car, you could drive downtown to the ice
plant instead of these neighborhood outlets. I made one
such trip myself when my Uncle Marshall Johns and his
family visited us in their old trap of a car from their farm
home in Johnson County.

We took the ice to my Aunt Bertha Anderson's house at
308 West White Street, and she even opened her glass
cabinet doors and set the table with Sunday-best goblets.
Moreover—at least once in my memory—she allowed us
to use her glass tea-stirrers and glass straws, the ultimate
in "class."

Mostly, though, we bought ice at Norman's. The ice
plant made deliveries to Mr. Norman's about twice a
week, bringing ice in big, hundred-pound blocks. These
big chunks were scored, so the storekeeper could easily,
with an ice pick, break them into twenty-five- and fifty-
pound pieces. A hundred-pound piece, if you could afford
one, cost forty cents.

For twenty cents you could buy fifty pounds, and for a
dime you could get twenty-five pounds. I don't know if
others did, but Mr. Norman would even split a twentyfive
pound chunk in two sections, which he sold for a nickel
apiece.

It was one of these twelve and one-half-pound blocks

that I bought, remembering Mom's final warning, "And don't let them sell you a little piece that's set there and melted all weekend."

As I held the tow sack open, a clerk carefully lowered the glistening prize. I immediately went to work, twisting the sack around and around as many times as it would go. Then I spread my old quilt out on the ground and wrapped it securely again. Finally, I wrapped it in the tarpaulin. By then it looked as big as a fifty-pound piece. Then, walking briskly, I pulled it home in Junior's wagon.

How miserly we were with that five-cent-piece-of-frozen-goodness, that oasis-creator in the midst of the scorched, Depression-ridden Illinois heartland.

After we had chipped off just the right amount for iced tea, it was my chore to rewrap the ice, crawl under the house where it was cool, and store it in a dark, moist corner. We stretched those nickel chunks for two or three days. If it came a cool, rainy snap, a chunk might last four days.

After dinner, Mom carefully washed the leftover ice from our glasses and put it in a small, brown pitcher for ice water or an afternoon lemonade. Never, never, never would you dream of throwing away a piece of ice just because it once cooled someone's glass of iced tea. Even when we cranked homemade ice cream, we carefully washed the salt away and used the ice again for something else.

Washing sugar from ice used in iced tea was especially painful to Mom. She often scolded Dad, who felt that tea was never truly sweetened unless about a half-inch of un-dissolved sugar stood in the bottom of his glass. Later, as times grew grimmer, she presweetened our tea while it was warm, making sure that every grain was dissolved.

I often wonder why iced tea doesn't taste as good to me today. Was it the way Mom brewed it, bringing her Lipton's tea to a boil, then quickly reducing the heat while it simmered on the back of the stove? Or did the taste of "real" ice add something missing from cubes?

I remember Dad complaining that watermelons "just don't taste like they did when I was a boy, when we grew our own, cut them in the patch, ate the hearts and threw the rest away." In contrast, I thought every melon we cut was the sweetest, juiciest, and ripest I had ever eaten.

And now here I am complaining that iced tea doesn't taste like it used to, just like he talked about watermelons. I don't understand this strange phenomenon, but I accept it as a fact of life. Maybe it's because the iced tea of my childhood reminds me how much I miss the caring mother who made it, my happiness her aim in every small task. Somehow, no other person on earth, however well-meaning, can fill that role. They can fill our glasses with tea and lemonade, but there's another emptiness they can never fill.

One summer about this time I visited my married sister, Mrs. Frank (Afton) Wolff, who lived in St. Louis. Frank worked for the Nelson Manufacturing Company, which made ice-cream cabinets for restaurants and drugstores. With his knowledge of refrigeration, Frank put together a homemade electric refrigerator. Using odds and ends of an old compressor, ice-cube trays, freon, and the like, he converted their ordinary icebox into an electric one.

Talk about heaven! I was there. That summer, we made tray after tray of popsicles with Kool-Aid. We could hardly wait for a tray to freeze, but started eating as soon as the red and orange cubes were mushy and icy. And this was an iced delicacy you ate right then, rather than recycling it for tomorrow.

Two housewives in our neighborhood had electric refrigerators—Mrs. John Wallace and Mrs. Walter Lang. About 1938, the Langs bought a new one from the Central

Illinois Public Service Company, where their daughter Melba had a steady job.

The Langs, a generous family, offered us their old one at a below-reasonable price. At that time, if you unplugged a refrigerator for any length of time, it was likely to "freeze up," whatever that meant. Unfortunately, the old refrigerator sat unplugged on their back porch for several days until Dad could get someone to help him carry it across the street. We moved it into our kitchen and plugged it in, but nothing happened. I can't describe our frustration—a jewel within our grasp, and we'd let it slip through our hands, partly due to carelessness.

I say it's hard to describe those hurts, for you must put yourself back in the thirties when money was so scarce that you preplanned every purchase. We planned to buy it—we didn't plan to spend as much again for repairs. But eventually we did, and it gave us years of useful service.

Several summers later, when I was in high school, I helped "Shorty" Strand sell snowcones at the county fairgrounds. Once or twice a day we drove down to the big ice plant where we scooped ice shavings by the shovels-full into washtubs (real sanitary!). For the first time, I saw ice being frozen in what looked to be 400-pound cylinders. It was like a midsummer's visit to the North Pole, a blizzard of frigidness.

But it was not nearly as tantalizing as my little nickel chunks of ice that I pulled home in Junior's wagon, back when it was hot enough to fry eggs on the sidewalk.

THE SHORT WAY TO KROGER'S

Bobby, I want you to take this five-dollar bill and go to Kroger's and get an order of groceries. Here's your list.

Now make sure they give you Swan's Down Cake Flour and no other brand—Eldon's birthday is coming up and I want to bake him an angel food cake. And ask for a large, firm head of cabbage. Feel of it to make sure it's hard, for that makes the best slaw. Soft heads are no good. And don't take a head with wilted leaves that's been in the bin all week.

In the late thirties, the Marion City Directory listed sixty grocery stores, ranging all the way from Norman's one-room store to the big Kroger and A & P outlets. Quite an assortment for a town of less than ten thousand population.

Like many families, we bought everyday groceries (milk, bread, ice, bananas, etc.) at the neighborhood stores. Every two weeks or so we'd "make an order" at Kroger's, taking advantage of their specials and lower prices. In fact, the growth of the chain stores eventually marked the end of the Mom and Pop stores, which couldn't compete with the big volume businesses.

For five dollars, you could buy more groceries than one person could carry—a couple of big boxes plus a sack or two. Since we had no car, and it was about a mile downtown to Kroger's, we managed different ways. Sometimes we rode with a neighbor, such as Ezra Davis or Myron Roberts, who had cars all during the Depression.

The simplest way was to buy your groceries, then call a cab, which for ten cents would take you and your foodstuffs to any address inside the city limits. For fifteen cents you could go as far as Spillertown or Dog Walk. Another way—once I got a bicycle—was to shop oftener and buy just what one sack would hold.

On this particular morning, I decided to take the shortcut to town, or at least it seemed shorter. I walked down to East Boulevard where I picked up the gravel path that skirted the city reservoir and brought me to the Illinois Central tracks, then west on the tracks to North Market where Kroger's was located.

Even if you never heard of my hometown, you may still enjoy that morning walk with me in the thirties. Since many small towns enjoy similarities, you may feel as if it's your own. We'll pay special attention to the stores.

Just a block from home I passed an empty half-lot at 1310 North State where once had stood Chicon's Pure Food Store. It was the forerunner of Guy Chicon Company, a wholesale grocery that has been in business in Marion since 1927.

Alicia, who is Guy's daughter, said it was the only retail store her father owned and that it was open only for a few years in the twenties. It was one of the first to advertise specials, at least in Marion. Alicia thinks the first special her dad advertised was sugar, which had been in short supply. The next morning, customers were lined up at the door, waiting for the store to open. And this at a small neighborhood grocery!

Alicia showed me a fascinating ad clipped from the February 8, 1923, issue of *The Marion Evening Post*. It advertised such specials as Rosedale Cling Peaches, Dream Oats, Bob White Corn Meal, Kirk's Flake Soap, Brass King washboards, No. 2 washtubs, and—fresh every Thursday—Acme cakes and crackers.

Amy Shotton Black, who grew up on North Glendale, remembers running over to Chicon's for candy as soon as her daddy came in from the mines. "Daddy had riders who paid him with a little change each day, which he'd give to us kids when he got home," she said. "I couldn't wait to get to Chicon's to spend mine."

When I reached the intersection of North State and East DeYoung, I could look to the left and see Will Travelstead's store at 303 East DeYoung. It was once owned by Herman and Sadie Garrison, who later relocated the store to 301 East Boulevard.

Mary (Garrison) Maidhof, their daughter, recalls as a little girl how she would run down the alley back of Ted Boles to Daddy's store for a lemon or whatever. "I have faint memories of dusting the cans and shelves and, occasionally, 'swiping' a piece of candy when Daddy wasn't looking," she told me.

Herman Garrison—a brother of spinster Vernie Garrison, a veteran first-grade teacher—was a storekeeper for fifty years, from 1919 to 1969. When he closed the doors for the last time in 1969, Sadie scooped up a handful of pennies from the cash register and dropped them in a little medicine bottle. Mary still keeps the bottle on a shelf in her home.

If you're still with me, we're now at Odom's Store at 1100 North State, also a Clover Farm affiliate, at one time owned by a Mr. York.

A little beyond this was a little store in the 900 block of North State; this store, which sat astride a creek, was once owned by Melvin Pulley. Past it, I soon reached the intersection of East Boulevard. It was here, again astride a creek, that Herman Garrison had his store. (By now I've identified three stores over creeks!) Looking to my left, at 300 East Boulevard, I could see the little red brick store once known as Hartwell's, and at other times as Perry's.

It was at Garrison's that I left the sidewalk and took a gravel path around the city reservoir, a short cut. I always enjoyed the walk beside the water and across the quaint, halfmoon concrete causeway that spanned the spillway. I liked the colorful leaves in the fall, the thin sheets of ice in the winter, the frogs croaking lazily in the spring, and fishermen on the banks in the summer.

This path brought me to the Illinois Central tracks, a highlight, for I liked to balance myself on one rail and see how far I could walk without falling off . . . or throw some of the big gravel rocks from the roadbed.

On the south side of the tracks, just short of North Market Street and the Illinois Central depot, was a water tower for the steam locomotives. The main line of the Illinois Central from Chicago to New Orleans passed through Carbondale to the west of Marion. A branch line to Marion brought, at one time, as many as three or four passenger trains a day, plus occasional freight and coal trains. The passenger trains then wound their way to such communities as Ozark, Brownfield, Golconda, Metropolis, Ulin, Cypress, and Joppa.

While passengers loaded and unloaded, the crew would uncouple the locomotive, which then chugged down to the water tank. Steam engines gulped hundreds of gallons of water, which was just as essential as the coal that fired the boilers. The water tank was made of wood. From it, the trainmen swung out to the engine a long, hinged, galvanized pipe through which the water flowed. The tower, or tank as it was commonly called, stood on legs on a concrete base.

During the thirties, the water tank was nicknamed the Hoover Hotel in honor of President Herbert Hoover, whom so many blamed for the Depression. Few people are aware that a new "hotel" opened in Marion during the thirties, when most construction came to a standstill. Tramps, or railroad hoboes, often spread their bedding on the concrete apron and slept there, partially sheltered from the rain and snow by the water tank above them.

Often I passed there at dusk and watched in awe as they fried fat meat and boiled coffee over an open fire. They made little tripods for pans to cook their simple rations. They were a motley group, dressed in long, shaggy overcoats, stocking caps, gloves with holes in the fingers, and shabby shoes often tied together with rags to keep the soles from falling off.

An unfulfilled wanderlust filled my breast.

"Now Bobby, when you pass those bums by the water tank, don't stop and talk," Mom often warned me. But Dad replied, "Now Ruby, those fellows wouldn't hurt no one. I've stopped and talked with them myself. They're ordinary fellows, down on their luck."

"I don't care," Mom countered, "it may be okay for you, but I don't think a boy has any business hanging around there. You can't tell what might happen."

I never had any real fear when I passed the Hoover Hotel, unless maybe it was dark enough to see those gaunt men silhouetted against their campfires. After all, I'd heard tales about gypsies and how they sometimes kidnapped little boys and girls, as well as stole chickens. You couldn't be too careful.

So I always walked on the far side of the tracks—close enough to see who were the latest boarders at the Hoover Hotel, but far enough away that I could run if I had to.

My Aunt Bertha Anderson, who lived near the tracks, fed many tramps during the thirties, usually on her back doorsteps. I can see one of them now, sitting sideways on a step, eating from a plate that rested on the porch, occasionally looking up with a furtive glance. Half-ashamed to beg—too hungry not to. If she had no leftovers, she'd fry a couple of eggs and garnish them with some cold biscuits and hot coffee.

"Bertha, don't you know those tramps mark your house?" friends asked solicitously. "You'll never be rid of them once they know you'll keep feeding them." (As a boy, I often looked for that "mark" that was supposedly on her house or at the curbside, but I never found one.)

"It doesn't pay me no mind," she'd say. "I'm not going to

turn anyone away that's hungry, if I know it." Sometimes they'd beg for a potato or piece of bacon, which they took back to cook and share with their buddies around the fire.

Safely past the Hoover Hotel I was now at North Market Street where I turned left. In a minute or two, I opened the door to Kroger Store No. 2 at 400 North Market, my grocery list in hand and the five-dollar bill crumpled up in my overall pockets.

It was the short way—and a good way—and I guess I walked it hundreds of times going to school, Saturday matinees, Sunday school, Kroger's, Woolworth's, and my Aunt Bertha's; which leads me to the next chapter describing another route to town.

THE LONG WAY TO KROGER'S

Now son, when you're done with your trading (shopping), walk down to Adams' Cab there in the same block and get them to bring you home with the groceries. The way I've figured, there'll be at least a dime left for your fare. And don't wait around, as the meat could spoil. Count your change and remember to put the bread on top so it won't get mashed.

I've described the shortest way to Kroger's for groceries. Now let me tell you about the long way.

Let's go out the back door at 1404 North State and cross the alley to North Glendale, then south to DeYoung. We'll miss the shortcut through the city reservoir, but there are two or three places of interest I want you to see along this route.

First, here's where Ezra and Lizzie Davis lived at 1314 North Glendale—the house with the wraparound porch that sits high over its basement on concrete blocks. The Davis and Hastings families were longtime friends. We visited back and forth one or two times a week, especially on Saturday nights to pop corn and listen to the Grand Ole Opry on radio WSM from Nashville, Tennessee.

The two women helped each other peel and can peaches, traded the latest news about who was expecting a baby and who had just got laid off work, and nursed each others' children when they were sick.

"Ruby, I want you to shut my mouth" was one of Lizzie's favorite sayings, used when Mom told her some neighborhood news that didn't always get in the newspapers.

The Davises heated their house with a coal furnace, which billowed up the heat from a central register (no duct work). "Kathryn, keep your dress down," Lizzie would warn her highschool daughter if we were there and she was standing over the register to get warm.

At one time, Lizzie ordered groceries from Sears. The problem was that you had to order by the case. Mom said that although Lizzie might save a few pennies that way, she just didn't want that much Sears-Roebuck pork and beans around the house at one time.

I don't know exactly what Ezra did for a living during the Depression. I know he worked a lot in his yard and garden, especially raising gladiolas, at which he was an expert. I suppose he was a miner. Lizzie, in contrast, lived like a perpetual whirlwind and made what money she could on the side, hanging and cleaning wallpaper, often for as little as one dollar a room.

What I remember most is Ezra's silence. When we'd drop in on Saturday nights, he'd be sitting at a small table rolling cigarettes, a week's supply. He said a gruff "Hello" and that was about it.

Ezra's chief pastime was membership in a fraternal

lodge known as Woodmen of the World. Once a week he put on his woodsman's uniform, shouldered an ax, and attended lodge meetings upstairs at 309 1/2 West Main. I remember going one night. The women and children sat in folding chairs around the walls. The men, axes on their shoulders, practiced marching drills in the big, open room. Each May 30, the Woodmen of the World marched in the Memorial Day parade from the public square out to the Rose Hill Cemetery. Ezra lived from one May 30 to the next.

Ezra died as quietly as he lived. One afternoon in the fifties, Lizzie came home and found him sitting in his customary chair, eyes fixed. He said nothing, for there was nothing to say. He was dead. Just as he caused little or no ripple on the ocean of life in our little world of Marion, Illinois, so he caused little ripple at his death.

I have no memory of Ezra ever speaking to me. Surely he did. What did he call me? Bobby? Son? I mention *Son* as it was a term of endearment my mother used for her three boys and other young men in the neighborhood. The word is locked forever in my memory chest of the thirties. "Son, I wouldn't do that if I were you . . . Son, I hope you will . . . I feel badly for you, Son . . . I'm sorry, Son, your daddy didn't get the job . . . We're all proud of you, Son."

Just a block down the street from Ezra's, let's walk slowly past the home of the late James H. Felts at 1216 North Glendale, where his widow still lived. It's a well-kept, two-story house with a wraparound porch, Victorian in architecture.

Mr. Felts had died in 1932 when I was eight years old, so I have little or no memory of him. Yet Mom spoke so often and admiringly of him that I felt I knew him. She often told how on the day of his funeral, she went to the First Baptist Church an hour early to get a seat.

In 1901, Mr. Felts cofounded the Egyptian Press Publishing Company, which in turn published *The Marion Evening Post*. From 1914 to 1918, he was a representative in the Illinois General Assembly from the fifty-first district, then a senator from the same district until his death. He bankrolled the first issues of *The Illinois Baptist* newspaper when it was founded in 1907, later serving briefly as its editor.

I was awed by this community leader—and to think that my mother was a good friend of his widow and sometimes went to their very house for meetings of her Baptist Ladies Aid circle!

In my mind, I contrasted Mr. Felts and Mr. Davis, who lived just a block apart yet were so far removed in culture, education, and influence. Being a miner's son, I identified with Ezra, even if he did pay me no mind. He was the kind of person my family felt comfortable around, for we were more like him.

But here was Senator Felts, too, living in the same neighborhood: the man who was for twenty-five years treasurer of the First Baptist Church; director of three banks; a publisher; a legislator who once turned down a share in a $100,000 bribe if he would vote wet. When he died, Lt. Gov. Fred E. Sterling actually appointed four senators to drive all the way from Springfield to Marion to represent the whole State of Illinois at his funeral; twenty editors and printers from neighboring towns served as honorary pallbearers.

In the thirties, these two men, so opposite in their roles, touched my life—one keeping my feet on the ground, the other inspiring me to stand on tiptoe. I thought about it at the time—although I couldn't verbalize it—as I pulled my borrowed wagon to Norman's for ice, as I walked to Swan's for minced ham, as I headed for Kroger's with a five-dollar bill in one pocket and a two-week list of groceries in the other.

And now, let's keep walking. Another block or so brings us to DeYoung. Here we cross the street and turn west past Swan's Store to a vacant lot at the southeast corner of DeYoung and Market.

Although in doing so I missed the home of Mr. Belford, who could have admitted me to the first grade when I was five *if he'd wanted to*, I always liked to cut through this vacant lot, then down and up the banks of a creek that flowed through it. Whatever the season, I liked to jump across that little stream, or step gingerly on stepping-stones, or in winter stomp my feet on the frozen ice.

Charles B. Garrigus, who in later years had a distinguished political and educational career in California and was also named poet laureate of that state, remembers the same shortcut. "As a boy, I lived on North Glendale for a couple of years," he told me. "I went to Swan's Store for walnettos and red hots and invariably cut across that same empty lot which, by the way, Mr. Swan owned. Well do I remember the time when he stretched a wire to keep out trespassers. I was in a hurry one night and ran into it. Knocked me down, left a big welt on my head."

As soon as you climbed the bank of the creek you were on North Market and, minutes later, passing Davis Brothers Motor Company at 700 North Market (where I saw the new cars but never dreamed anyone ever bought one, even Mr. Swan).

A partner, Kenneth Davis, made frequent buying trips to St. Louis. A fast driver, he often boasted how quickly he could make it to Marion. Seems to me it was three hours. That's not too fast today but in the early thirties, with narrow highways and twisting routes through East St. Louis and Belleville, plus numerous smaller communities, it was a dare-deviling claim.

He didn't complete his last trip, though: he died in a crash on the Eads Bridge while crossing the Mississippi River into Illinois.

But fast cars were not part of my world—I was on foot to Kroger's, which I reached soon thereafter.

A SACK OF BREAD AT BERTHA'S

Bobby, on your way home from school, stop at Bertha's house. I'll bet she has a peck of bread saved for the chickens.

My Uncle Charley and Aunt Bertha Anderson did their share to keep the neighborhood grocery stores open during the thirties. On the days during the Depression when Uncle Charley wasn't working (and that was most of the time), his life began with a morning ritual. That ritual consisted of reading the St. Louis *Globe-Democrat*, then going to Weinacht's Grocery, Sander's Market, Bob Wanless' Store, or Flukes' Market.

Aunt Bertha set a fine table, even during the worst of the bad times, and Uncle Charley was a familiar sight, about ten o'clock each morning, coming down the sidewalk with a brown sack of that day's groceries under his arm.

Bertha was the oldest of my mother's three sisters, the other two being Alverta and Mattie. She first married Marshall Jack. As a boy, I remember her telling how she started housekeeping in a two-room, sparsely furnished cottage out near Dog Walk (now known as Cedar Grove).

"Marshall and I had practically nothing, the barest of furniture, but those were my happiest days," she often reminisced in typical "good old days" style. Their two

The author, aged two months, in a buggy behind the family store, July 1924. This is the only known photo of the Hastings' store.

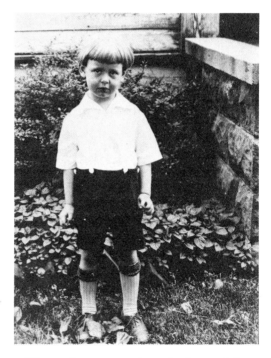

The author at age three, in front of the family home.

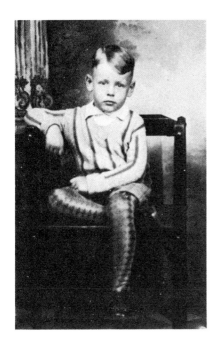

The author at age four. The date was 1928, one year before the Great Depression.

The author's father, Eldon Hastings, from the 1930s.

The author's mother, Ruby Hastings, late 1930s. The supports for the armrests of the chair were salvaged from the gingerbread decorations for the porch. The dog's name was Jerry; an ice card hangs in the window.

Eldon Hastings, 1949. He is shown with some of the products in the W. T. Raleigh line, which he sold for twenty-five years.

*Eldon and Ruby
Hastings, 1956.*

The family home at 1404 North State, 1959.

children were Cecil and Lela. Cecil died in a mysterious accident or explosion on a barge where he was working on the Mississippi River. This was a closed subject and I never asked questions.

Then one morning she fixed the dinner bucket for Marshall, her miner-husband, and by midday, fellow workers knocked at her door to say that he was dead, a victim of the all-too-frequent mine accidents in southern Illinois.

By the time I came along she was married to Charley Anderson. They lived in a corner house at 108 West White, just a block off of North Market and back of the Davis Motor Company.

Aunt Bertha was much like a second mother. It was only slightly out of my way to stop there on my way to school, to church, or to town. I was there two or three times a week and felt as free to open the door and go in unannounced as I did at home. She was always treating me to snacks, and during the winter I enjoyed sitting by their open grate.

In the winter, they heated only two rooms, unless they were expecting company. These were the kitchen and the dining, or sitting, room. A coal cookstove and a coal-burning, smoky fireplace (or grate as they called it) provided heat for these two rooms, the others being closed off. I can still feel the chill of their unheated bedrooms when I stayed overnight during the winter. But my aunt had access to an unending stack of heavy, homemade quilts, which she kept piling on until at last I was warm, even if I felt as if my breath were smashed out of me.

A swing and lawn chairs graced the front porch, and here they spent many hours during the summer. On a typical August morning I would ride my bicycle into their front yard, then walk up the steps and sit with them on the porch. On the opposite corner, the grinding machines of the Thurmond Monument Company would be at work.

Back then, granite for gravestones came in big slabs. Firms such as Thurmond's cut the big slabs into smaller pieces, then polished and lettered them to order, with the name, birthdate, etc., of the deceased. The saws, the air chisels, the grinders, and the polishers—all gave off a distinctive hum and whir, which I can still hear. Apparently, folks kept dying and their relatives continued to buy tombstones, even during the Depression.

Uncle Charley, an ardent Republican, blamed Franklin D. Roosevelt for every ill that befell mankind, including the Depression. You would have thought he shredded the St. Louis *Globe-Democrat* (a Republican paper) for breakfast cereal each morning. He began each day by devouring the paper, arming himself with editorial quotes and statistics so he could debate anyone he met on the public square or in the grocery stores.

In his book, *Travels with Charley*, John Steinbeck quotes a Minnesota storekeeper who in turn was describing a friend by the name of Larren. He said, "Why, I remember when people took everything out on Mr. Roosevelt. Andy Larren got red in the face about Roosevelt one time when he had the croup."

It's not much of an exaggeration to say that my uncle could also blame a bad cough on the Democratic president who, in his opinion, created the joblessness and all the "crazy" alphabet efforts to put the country on its feet, including the WPA, NRA, CCC, and PWA.

He continued to lay the world's guilt on Roosevelt, right on through World War II. As far as he was concerned, Roosevelt led the bombing raid on Pearl Harbor that ushered the United States into war. He even had some kind of a grudge against Falla, the president's little dog. When FDR died on April 12, 1945, it was a unique loss for Uncle Charley—he had lost his whipping boy!

I don't know what my aunt and uncle lived on during the Depression. I know he worked very little. But then, they had few expenses. They were in relatively good health, had their house paid for, spent nothing for furniture and the bare minimum for clothing, didn't own a car, paid no income tax, disconnected their party-line telephone, took no vacations, never ate in restaurants, bought only enough fuel to heat two rooms, and never heard of air conditioning.

Food was the one item they refused to economize on. Not that they were extravagant, but they insisted on quality meats and the like.

After Uncle Charley digested the morning paper, he might walk around the corner to Weinacht's Grocery and buy a choice piece of steak. I was in Mr. Weinacht's Store on North VanBuren occasionally, but seldom did I see another customer. It was absolutely the tiniest store I was ever in. How he made a living, I don't know. His specialty was meat, and it was there the Andersons went if they wanted a good roast or thick pork chops.

Mostly, Uncle Charley traded at Flukes' Market at 412 North Market. Flukes' prices and quality were higher than many stores in Marion, and Aunt Bertha felt their foodstuffs were worth the extra cost. Flukes' catered to the higher-income folks in Marion, some of whom even telephoned in their grocery orders for later delivery in the day—something my parents would never have dreamed of doing.

Since Aunt Bertha baked hot bread twice a day, and didn't believe in leftovers, she always had generous amounts of cornbread and biscuits to dispose of. This surplus bread she saved for us to use as chicken feed, keeping it in a meal or flour sack. So whenever I stopped at 108 West White, I knew to bring home the sack of bread. We kept chickens in a pen in our backyard, and Dad would crumble up the old bread and feed it to them.

Snapshots of my aunt from the twenties show her as a tall, erect, well-dressed woman, proud of her long hair and nice clothing. The Depression robbed her of some of this. I doubt if she bought one new dress from 1930 to 1940. She made do with what she had, appearing to splurge only on the food she set on her table.

For a short period during the thirties, she and Mom refused to speak to each other or to visit. I don't know why—maybe the fallout of an argument between Dad and Charley on the public square one day that ended in a shoving match. During that time, I continued to drop in at the Andersons, the same as if it were my home. But it was a strained relationship, because they got to writing notes back and forth to each other, using me as a messenger boy.

It was distasteful and I didn't like it, although I dutifully delivered the notes back and forth. Their spat probably didn't last over a week or so, but to me it seemed endless. I wondered if all our good times might end over something so trivial. However, they were soon reconciled and I never heard another word about the episode. I'm sure both were embarrassed over the whole thing and anxious for bygones to be bygones.

Toward the end of my high-school days and after I'd announced my dreams to be a minister, Aunt Bertha would often greet me, "Why here comes Dr. Throgmorton!" She did so good-naturedly, referring to a former pastor of the First Baptist Church in Marion, W. P. Throgmorton, who had married my parents and baptized my mother.

Coincidentally, I later served seventeen years as editor of *The Illinois Baptist*, a weekly newspaper that Dr. Throgmorton founded in Marion in 1907. Was she prophetic?

If I stopped by on my way to church on Sunday mornings, as likely as not Aunt Bertha was making two lemon meringue pies. She specialized in lemon pies. Her crust was always crisp and flaky, the meringue stood high and fluffy, and the lemon filling was so firm and full of body that you could slice it with a fork. "If it's anything I won't stand in my kitchen, it's a runny pie," she often said.

And in the dining room, Uncle Charley would be shaving, a weekly ritual. Actually, it was a major expedition, not a mere ritual. When he shaved, it meant big steaming pots of hot water, plus layers and layers of newspapers spread on the dining-room table for his pans, shaving mug, brushes, and razor. Then came the endless sharpening of his razor as he whopped, whopped, whopped on a big, black strap. And finally, the long, slow deliberate strokes on his face and fat jowls that drooped below his chin.

"Charley Anderson can use more hot water, waste more soap, and take longer to do it than any man in Marion," Bertha would comment. "You mind the lemon pies and I'll mind the shaving," he would counter.

Sometimes we visited the First Methodist Church with her on Sunday nights. As a boyhood treat to buffer a long sermon, she fished around in her purse for a stick of Teaberry chewing gum. Somehow, whenever I see a Methodist church today, I think of Teaberry gum.

At the corner of their lot stood a huge cherry tree. It was so big that I never dreamed it was a cherry tree until one spring when it exploded with bright blossoms. It was the talk of the neighborhood. I don't know how many years had gone by without that tree bearing a single cherry. Then right in the heart of the Depression, it bore abundantly, far more than the Andersons could pick and use.

Word spread about "that big tree loaded with cherries" in Charley Anderson's yard. They invited anyone to come and pick without charge. Tucked in my memory chest is a mental photo of ladders lying in their yard and propped against the tree, eager neighbors filling their buckets and, most of all, a feeling of prosperity and abundance, at least of cherries, and all for free.

That burgeoning cherry tree was, to me, like the first rainbow that Noah saw following the Flood. As the rainbow was a promise that the earth would never again be deluged with water, so the cherry tree was a promise to us that God had not deserted his people, even in Marion, and that some day food would again be abundant and there would be jobs for all who wanted to work.

Another vivid memory, dating to about 1940, is a long line of men at an employment office on North Market, just around the corner from the Andersons. The Sherwin-Williams Corporation had been awarded a contract to build a bomb-loading plant between Marion and Carbondale. I was amazed to watch the long line of applicants actually being hired for real jobs that paid real money.

Previously, I had seen only long relief lines or men in lines along the highways, down in the ditches, working on WPA (a government make-work program).

Fortunately, Uncle Charley was hired as a night security guard at the new plant. I was in high school and Aunt Bertha often asked me to stay with her at night, as she was afraid by herself. I was pleased to do so for it meant a shorter walk to school, as well as her famed hot biscuits for breakfast.

I remember Uncle Charley as he dressed for work on winter nights. Heavy boots and socks, layers and layers of woolen shirts and tops. By the time he left for another night's work walking the perimeter of the plant, he looked like Santa Claus. I shared his sense of pride and well-being, his emotional satisfaction in knowing a regular paycheck was coming in.

Somehow, I picked up these good feelings from men as they began to get jobs, even though it meant little to me personally. "Glad to hear you got on out at the plant," friends might say, even if they were still jobless. It was a hope, a dream, that before long everyone would be back at work; that you could install a telephone again; buy a new dress; open the doors and let the heat go all the way to the back bedroom; maybe afford a stick of real butter in place of oleo.

Aunt Bertha didn't live to be an old woman. I think of her as a person who preferred what she considered a good life in lieu of a longer life. When she learned she was a diabetic, she refused to alter her diet and was irregular, at best, with inoculations of insulin. "I'm going to enjoy the food I've always liked, as long as I live," she often said.

Before her death, she left instructions for her family not to bury her in a vault. She was reconciled to her body returning to the earth. Her daughter Lela followed her wishes, but later regretted it.

Aunt Bertha died in her own bed at home, surrounded by neighbors and her three sisters, with little fanfare and no heroic, expensive, life-prolonging measures.

It was a late winter afternoon in 1946 when she died. I was in Ft. Worth in school. Mom was there and the same afternoon wrote me a moving letter describing Aunt Bertha's last moments. How I wish I had saved that letter. I can't begin to reconstruct it, but it conveyed to me the feeling that things were just the way Aunt Bertha wanted them.

Her soul didn't have to be pried away from her body— she went gently and willingly.

In these days of medical expertise when we hold on to life as if there was nothing beyond, and spend thousands of dollars to extend one life for a few days of weeks, I think of my Aunt Bertha. To her, the world wasn't something to hold on to at all costs. She could take life, including the tragic deaths of her son and first husband. She could take the Depression and the crimp it put in her lifestyle, the faded cotton dresses, the blank place on the wall where the telephone once hung. She could also take what money they had and set a good table, including lemon pies with the best ingredients.

And then, when the time came, she could turn loose of all of it.

We're always telling each other to "hold on" and "never give up." One legacy of the Great Depression was that you also learned to let go. "For we know that if our earthly house of *this* tabernacle were dissolved, we have a building of God, an house not made with hands, eternal in the heavens" (2 Corinthians 5:1).

AN UNBROKEN THREAD

Eldon, I've got an idea. We can keep the store open, even if we are quarantined. Me and the kids will stay in the house, and I'll fix you a cot in the store. You can come to the back door for your meals, which I'll have ready on a tray.

In the early 1920s, Dad built a one-room grocery store on the same ninety-foot lot where our house stood. The store, with two gasoline pumps in front, stood to the north of our house out near the sidewalk.

Work in the coal mines was always on a piecemeal, part-time basis. Keeping the store gave Dad something to do when the mines were shut down. When the mines worked, Mom kept the store. It was strictly a Mom and Pop family enterprise, drawing customers from a three to four block radius.

Once, even though my older brothers and sister were quarantined with scarlet fever and chicken pox, my parents managed to keep the store open. Dad slept in a cot in the store, and Mom took care of the kids. At mealtime she would set his tray on the back steps for him to carry out to the store. After eating, he set the dirty dishes back on the steps.

The story of that quarantine was handed down in our family like a legend. Each family member was proud of the cooperative effort, although to others it may seem a trivial episode in the great, ongoing march of history.

Since I was not born until 1924, the store was on its last legs by the time I can remember.

Glenn Travelstead, who was born next door at 1406 North State, and lives there to this day, remembers buying groceries there as late as 1929. "It was a little one-room store, not much bigger than a garage," Glenn told me. "At the front were two display windows and a small porch. And on the south was a side door. But in 1930 or 1931, your dad sold it and had it torn down and moved away."

As the chain stores grew and folks bought cars, the little stores started to close, one by one, since families could go where prices were cheaper. The 1929 Depression was the final blow to Hastings' Store.

I remember the credit or sales books that Dad kept for each customer. Long after the store closed, he frequently leafed through them. Many showed unpaid balances for customers whom he had carried through lean times. But he showed no bitterness that I recall. As work petered out, the miners had little cash to buy today's groceries, let alone pay for last month's.

Once the store closed, I often played inside, turning the old-time coffee mill and sipping imaginary bottles of soft drinks. I also played with the quart glass containers, which looked like milk bottles, once used to dispense motor oil into cars. A metal spout screwed on the top of these bottles, which were refilled and used over and over.

I remember a square place in our lawn where the ground sank after the gasoline storage tank was dug up. It reminded me of a new grave.

I have one or two faint memories of watching for customers while Mom ran into the house on an errand. I was to tell them she would be right back. Since business was so slow, I doubt if I ever had anyone to tell she'd be back soon!

Mom and Dad were married on March 17, which was also Dad's birthday. One March we set up long tables on saw horses in the store and enjoyed a big birthday and anniversary dinner. My dad's relatives arrived, laden with favorite dishes.

And so we feasted in a vacant building, haunted with memories of better days. But since we turned more than one lemon into lemonade, we enjoyed the dinner as if we were in a great banquet hall of some ancient castle—and, in quieter moments, wondered about tomorrow.

Those revelers I remember best are Lee and Eddie Hartwell; Ted and Flossie Boles and Helen; Archie and Elva Rodd, Charles and Kenneth; Elbert and Flora Bain; Winnie Hamlet and Loren; Troy and Bertie Bradley; John and Annie Sharp; Mary Roberts; Dialtha James; and Ellen Carter, who made a little pin money by selling Saymon Salve and other products from her home.

A poignant memory reaches back to one fall day, just before the store closed. It was rainy and turning cold. Mom and I sat around the coal stove in the back of the store, hoping for a customer. Occasional thunder rumbled across the fall skies. "That's just 'tater wagons, crossing an old wooden bridge," Mom reassured me. And to this day, I hear 'tater wagons when it thunders.

In the back alley we heard another wagon, creaking under the weight of a load of coal. "Your daddy borrowed a horse and wagon and went out to Spillertown for some coal," Mom continued. "That's him now. He thinks he can lay in enough to do us all winter."

"Enough to do us all winter!" Only six words, but so full of promise, of warmth, of security.

When children hear their parents talking about hard times, they can imagine things worse than they are. But that morning, all the fear of a cold winter rode off in 'tater wagons, rumbling across wooden bridges.

In earlier years, Dad and my maternal grandfather, J. H. Gordon, were partners in a store on East Boulevard. I know it was there in 1916, for my sister, Afton, started the first grade at the nearby Jefferson School that year. She remembers stopping at Grandpa's "big store on Boulevard."

Erby Hastings, one of Dad's nephews, often told how he worked there as a teenager. Competition was keen among the many stores in the neighborhood. So Erby arrived as early as 5:00 A.M., then went door to door soliciting orders. Later in the day, he delivered the groceries in a buggy.

Knock on someone's door at five o'clock in the morning? Remember these were the days when Marion miners rose early to catch interurban trains to mines at Herrin, Energy, and Carterville. This often meant long walks to the mines. Many set their alarms for 3:30 or 4:00, which explains how door-to-door sales could start before sunup.

About 1917, J. H. and Sarah Gordon moved back to Johnson County, where they'd raised a family, and opened a country store.

It was at the foot of the hill as you approached Bethlehem General Baptist Church and Bethlehem School. That's about seven miles northeast of Goreville and twelve miles southwest of Marion. The store was more like a shed than anything else. There he sold such staples as flour, meal, coffee, sugar, spices, vinegar, coal oil (kerosene), and a few patent medicines.

A wholesaler called on him once a month. But in bad weather, the salesman offered Grandpa Gordon three dollars to meet him in Goreville. "Grandpa would drive his buggy to Goreville to pick up his orders at the Central and Eastern Illinois Railroad depot," my cousin Loren Johns remembers.

Hazel Bradley, who lived just over a field from the store, remembers it. "I walked across that field many a time when the roads were too bad to get to Marion or Creal Springs," she told me. "Your grandpa was so proud of that little store with its potbellied stove in the middle, a counter, and shelves around the walls. Menfolk liked to loaf there in bad weather. We had our own milk and eggs, but we went there for staples, needles and pins, home remedies, and the like."

My sister, Afton, remembers the curtains in Grandma Gordon's home next door. "Believe it or not, Grandma made curtains out of ordinary newspapers," she told me, "even cutting neat little fringes at the bottom."

I have two mementoes from these little stores. One is a wooden box in which bulk coffee was shipped to Dad's store. Some of the original brown covering paper with bright red lettering, "Schottens Coffee," is still intact.

The other is a two-drawer spool cabinet from Grandpa's store in town. "Clark's O. N. T." it reads on the front, standing for "Our New Thread," manufactured by Coats and Clark, Inc. Rats have gnawed on one of the drawers— an effort to filch thread to make nests?

Grandpa took it with him to Johnson County, where he used it for a "cash register" to keep his change! Years later, when I began to write, my mother used the same cabinet to file my first articles.

Forgive the pun, but there's an unbroken thread to the present in that old spool cabinet, in spite of the rats!

TWO LOAVES OF TWIN BREAD

*Yes, you can have another banana. Here, let me cut this
ripest one at the top of the stalk. But I think you've eaten
enough of those coconut macaroon cookies for one day.*

Before we close the door for the last time on Dad's store
on North State, and dig up the gas tank, and sweep the
grounds from the coffee mill, and move out the wooden
counters and the glass candy case, and cut down the final
banana stalk with its two or three remaining pieces of
fruit, blackened and shriveled, let's take one more look
out the front door.

Down the Spillertown hard road, which begins where
North State ends, I see, on her way to town, a small,
slightly stooped, elderly woman—at least she looks elderly to a four-year-old. She walks slowly but steadily,
looking neither to the left nor right, indifferent to the
heat or cold. In two or three hours, she'll be back, carrying
a shopping bag in her left hand. And on the return trip
she will fold her right arm closely at her back (the way
one would if trying to scratch an inaccessible spot). Every
so often she will stop to shift the heavy brown bag to her
right hand, then lift her left arm to her back.

"Why does she hold one arm at her back?" I asked Dad.
"That gives her balance, helps to rest you on a long walk,"
he explained. I told myself that when I got old and had to
walk three or four miles to town and back, I'd fold my
arms like that and it wouldn't seem far.

Glenn Travelstead thinks her name was Issler. I don't
know. She was just one of those shadowy figures that you
draw up from your childhood and wonder who they really
were, where they were going, what they were thinking as
they trudged step after step into your life, and then out
again.

At times, I'd go all the way out to the street curb to look down what we called the Spillertown hard road (an expression for the first paved roads). In the distance I saw strip-mine hills. Everyone knew gypsies lived in those hills. And little boys like me knew they sometimes rode by in their covered wagons and kidnapped youngsters who wandered too far out in the street.

Occasionally a black boy, about ten years old, came down that hard road. Neat, courteous, nice-looking, he seldom glanced at us. What's strange about that? Nothing, except no black people that I knew of lived in Spillertown—or anywhere in Marion—except in the south end known as Jent's Addition.

Whose child was he? Where did he live? What would he do in town? When he was about thirteen, he died under mysterious circumstances, maybe drowned. I had lots of questions, but I never asked.

As best I can understand my own feelings, I was never prejudiced against other races. A number of foreign-born lived in Marion, attracted to southern Illinois by jobs in the mines. Occasionally someone would refer to "Dago Town," a section where a few Italian families lived. Or my Uncle Charley Anderson would call a miner from England a Johnnie Bull.

Although the black children had their own grade school, our high school was integrated. However, black students were made to sit in the back of classrooms, especially in the big assembly hall where we were assigned permanent seating for study periods.

I felt the blacks were singled out under the watchful eye of whatever teacher might be monitoring the study hall. The teacher on duty sat at a high desk at the back of the hall, within easy reach of the blacks. A white student down front might get away with talking or moving about, but the black students were kept on a tight rein.

The 1939 edition of the Marion City Directory has a revealing footnote: "Married women engaged in some responsible occupation are listed separately. . . . Colored persons are shown by ©. The publishers are very careful in using this designation but do not assume any responsibility in case of error."

One wonders about "irresponsible occupations" of women, if any, and why the blacks were singled out. If someone such as my boyhood friend, James O. Dungey, had bright red hair, why not put an ® after his name?

Christ's teachings about the equality of all peoples have been slow to penetrate society. But more and more we see the truth of Galatians 3:28: "There is neither Jew nor Greek, there is neither bond nor free, there is neither male nor female: for ye are all one in Christ Jesus."

Now back to Hastings' Store. Let's look out the front windows to the Walter Lang home at 302 East Clark. This was a fascinating family to me. I idolized their four almost grown children, then still at home.

The identical twin boys, Pete and Bill, were athletic, and scraped the sod for their own tennis court on a vacant lot between us and them. I often sat on the street curb and chased stray balls. A third son, Leland, as well as their daughter Melva, were also friends of my brothers and sister.

In the late twenties, the older neighborhood boys built what they called "The Hut" on another vacant lot next to us. They first erected four corner posts, then nailed on old tin roofing for the walls and top. They dragged up an old linoleum for the floor and even put in a little wood-burning stove. They furnished it with a sagging sofa and odds and ends of chairs. To me, it was a magic mansion.

But "The Hut" was strictly off-limits to youngsters my age. I suspected that things went on inside that little boys shouldn't see. One December 31, they sat up to "watch the old year go out." I wanted so badly to join them, but I was put to bed at a decent hour. I wondered how the old year looked as he "went out." Did he slip out down the alley or walk boldly down State Street, old but proud? I was left wondering. I still don't know.

Pete remembers his parents were still using kerosene lamps when Dad's store opened. "Potatoes were so cheap then that when I went over for a can of coal oil, we just used a small potato to plug the spout," he told me.

Pete and Bill were not the real names of the twins. Walter, their dad, nicknamed them and it stuck for life. Many neighbors couldn't tell them apart. But I soon learned that Pete's face was thinner, so I always knew which was which.

Walter was a skilled carpenter, but I remember him working little during the Depression. He raised bird dogs and liked to hunt. When he wanted to go uptown and loaf on the public square, he often leaned on a rural mailbox and thumbed a ride with someone coming from Spillertown.

Mrs. Lang was the hardest-working woman I knew. Other women might finish their day's work and sit on their front porches. Not her. She was an excellent seamstress, and big cars would pull up in front with ladies who paid her to make their dresses, suits, and blouses. She not only took in sewing and did housework for four children, but in later years had the care of Walter, who developed palsy.

Walter blamed Sheriff Oren Coleman for his palsy. According to Glenn Travelstead, here's what happened. Walter was downtown the day that depositors were making a run on one of the banks, just before it failed. Coleman later testified that Walter was shoving or otherwise creating a nuisance, so he knocked him down with a blackjack or maybe the butt of his pistol. Walter claims his hands and arms trembled from that day forward.

Walter sued the sheriff and they had a jury trial in the

Williamson County courthouse. The jury found Coleman
guilty, but awarded Walter a judgment of only one dollar.
I suppose they felt each was at fault. Anyway, Walter
framed that one-dollar bill and joked about it for years.

Whether the blow triggered the palsy, I don't know. I do
know it worsened until the time came when his entire
body trembled. In the summertime, he sat under the trees
in a homemade lawn chair with rockers. At times he
would motion for me to cross the street and help him up.
Mom often said that if no one were around, Walter could
rock the chair with the motion of his own body, then get
up unassisted. I don't know. I do know the Langs would do
anything for us.

As an example, they had one of the two telephones in
our neighborhood. I often knocked and asked if I could
"borrow your phone." They were always gracious. Once or
twice during the thirties when we "got bad news on long
distance," they waked us at night. You never dialed a toll
call just for fun. It was for emergencies only, and the mere
word that "you have a long-distance call" triggered a sus-
penseful fear in the pit of your stomach.

Pete Lang has long since gone home with his last can of
kerosene, but let's look at one more customer before clos-
ing the door for good.

The other home in our neighborhood with a telephone
was the John Wallace family, who lived in a big white
stucco house atop a rolling incline on the Spillertown
hard road. But you would no more ask to use their telephone than you would call the White House and invite
yourself to dinner.

The Wallaces were the only people we knew with two
bathrooms, two cars, and a power mower. Also, John was
the only man I knew who worked every day during the
Great Depression.

John and George Wallace were brothers who came from
Ohio to Illinois and formed the Wallace Coal Company. I

believe they sunk more than one mine, including the New Virginia Mine northeast of Marion, which managed to stay open during the thirties. You could set your watch by when John left for work. He was methodical and hard-working, although he looked straight ahead when he passed our house and seldom bothered to speak. (Traffic in the thirties was slow enough that it was customary to wave or smile at someone you knew.) Yet his management skills kept his mine open when others were failing, and he created jobs for those who otherwise might have been on welfare.

John and Alice Wallace had two sons—J. K. and Dawson. J. K. was a medical student at the University of Illinois—another unheard of thing in our neighborhood. Dawson was my age. Neighborhood boys would tease him when he came to our store and asked for "two ten-penny loaves of twin bread." Due to a slight speech impediment which he soon outgrew, Dawson had trouble with the words *two* and *ten* and *twenty*. He twisted them around somehow, although Dad always knew what he meant.

Dawson and I played together, usually in his yard or barn. He didn't enjoy the run of the neighborhood like the other kids. He kept busy at home riding his pony, running the power mower, or caring for their goats.

I remember going inside to play only one time. He showed me his big electric train set, spread out all over one room. How I envied him and wanted to go back again and again. But it was more like a train on display in a museum, to look at, rather than touch.

I felt the same about David and Lloyd Schafale's lead soldier collection. David and Lloyd, schoolmates of mine, lived at 503 East Boulevard. They melted their own lead and poured it into molds, casting all kinds of little soldiers. When Lloyd gave me one I was so proud, yet dreamed of how wonderful it would be to make all you wanted. I could see hundreds—maybe thousands—of lead soldiers marching across the dressers and shelves of the Schafale brothers' bedroom, then spilling out all over the floor.

Alice Wallace was obsessed with cleanliness. Some neighbors gossiped that if she didn't have enough laundry to fill the clothesline on Monday mornings, she'd pull clean linens out of dresser drawers to wash. Others said she changed their bed sheets every day and that they never, never used a towel more than once.

Mrs. Wallace, like many mothers of the thirties, was solicitous about Dawson's health. She constantly suspected he might be coming down with something! My mother was the same way. But you must remember that those were days when smallpox, scarlet fever, diphtheria, and whooping cough still put fear in the hearts of parents. Two of my classmates, Bobby Love and Bobby Lowe, died of scarlet fever while we were in grade school. Antibiotics and other so-called miracle drugs were unknown.

If you had a "peaked" look, if your tongue was coated, if you were white around the mouth, or if you appeared flushed with fever when your Mom held the back of her hand to your forehead, you needed doctoring.

I often wondered why God created castor oil. The name of my favorite soft drink was called Whistle. But Mom almost ruined it for me by first giving me a tablespoon of castor oil, followed by a big drink of Whistle. And all the time she would be saying, like a barker at the country fair, "Step right up folks, get your ice cold soda here, just a nickel, cold and sweet; there son, drink it all in one swallow!"

For some reason, Mrs. Wallace concluded that something ailed Dawson. True, he was thin, somewhat frail as a small boy, and had lots of bad colds. But in general, he appeared healthy to me. Mom entertained her own opinion—"Mrs. Wallace washes him to death."

Dr. Zach Hudson, the company doctor for the Wallace

Coal Company, advised Alice to give Dawson goat's milk. So they bought not one goat but an entire herd. He also said Dawson needed more sunlight. I remember the summer Mrs. Wallace cut off all his shirt sleeves at the shoulder. Lots of boys ran around with no shirt. At least he got his arms in the sun.

About every other year, Mrs. Wallace got a new Hudson for her personal car. She was very generous with rides to school for neighborhood kids. How neat to step in a new-like car and be whisked off to school! It gave you a feeling of opulence, like eating real whipped cream on your jello.

I don't know why she refused to allow Dawson to walk to school with other youngsters. Religiously, she chauffeured him every morning and every evening. Sometimes after school, Mrs. Wallace would drive downtown and let Dawson out of the car. "Go up to the mine office and get your daddy's paycheck," she'd say.

How marvelously strange were those words during the Depression, especially in the ears of a boy whose father earned dribbles here and there—but never a paycheck!

Yet there was a commonness about this family, even if at times they appeared to be aloof.

In the fall of 1938, Mom got a job in the junior high school lunchroom. She fried hamburgers and boiled hot dogs for the students, then cooked a home-style meal for the faculty, who ate last.

We still had no car, so for several months Mrs. Wallace was kind enough to give her a ride each morning. Mom would get out at Kroger's on North Market where she placed an order for the day's groceries, then walked over to Washington School.

On the third anniversary of my brother LaVerne's death, Mom sent a dollar to the Baptist Hour program heard every morning from seven until eight on radio WEBQ in Harrisburg. Along with the dollar was a request for a hymn to be dedicated in memory of LaVerne. That was a common custom, and the name of the deceased would be read on the air.

"I hope Mrs. Wallace doesn't come before they read LaVerne's name," Mom said to me. "If she does, could you run out and ask her to wait just a minute?"

I hesitated to ask her. When LaVerne died in 1936, neighbors and relatives crowded into our home and some sat up all night, as the custom was. Not long afterwards, wakes were moved to funeral homes. But in the mid-thirties, families still brought their dead to their homes for mourning and visitation.

I have no memory of Alice or John coming to express their sympathy. Maybe they did. If so, it was brief and formal. And I remember the afternoon of the funeral, as the processional was preparing to leave for the First Baptist Church downtown.

When we walked out the front door and down the steps to the waiting cars, it seemed to me that every neighbor in the north end of Marion was standing in our yard and on the sidewalks. But I have no memory of seeing the Wallaces. And now we were asking Mrs. Wallace to wait on us.

I'll always remember her kind, soft answer. "Tell Ruby not to rush. We have time."

In a minute or two Mom hurried out to the car, breathing deeply. "Thank you, Alice. I got to hear his name."

And then we drove silently down the street.

A TRIP TO WEST FRANKFORT

Ruby, I've got these warrants from West Side Mine. If we could take them to the Coal Field Store in West Frankfort, they might allow us something, maybe 50 per cent or more. Ezra Davis said he'd drive us up there.

Dad's last job before the Great Depression was at the West Side Mine in West Frankfort, twelve miles north of Marion. Several companies tried to make a go of West Side. It would start up, then shut down. Start up, then shut down.

West Side finally heaved one last sigh, then died for good. Dad came home saying it was all over. As I recall, management could pay the miners little or nothing for their final few days of work. The money just wasn't there. This may have been the time Dad came home with warrants, or promises, that the mine might someday make good.

Warrants were common in the thirties, especially from county governments. Schoolteachers of that era can remember being paid in scrip or warrants. In turn, they took these to banks or stores to redeem them. Some paid in face value. Others were discounted from ten cents to ninety cents on the dollar. Much depended on the faith a retailer or bank placed in the organization that issued them.

This probably explains why Mom, Dad, and I made a buying trip to the Coal Field Store in West Frankfort, where we could trade the warrants for food or other products. I sensed in my parents a subdued gaiety, a child-like joy at being able to redeem for some amount what at first seemed worthless.

As we approached the outskirts of West Frankfort on Route 37, the tipple of West Side Mine, on our left, stood gaunt and dark against the evening sky. We turned right onto East Main where two company stores were open for business.

One, a grocery store, was operated by the Chicago, Wilmington, and Franklin Coal Company (C. W. & F. Co.). The other, known as the Coal Field Store, was owned by the Old Ben Coal Corporation. Located in the 400 block of East Main, Coal Field was more like a department store, as it stocked furniture and clothing as well as groceries.

*Matthews General Store, near Pinckneyville, about 1918.
Drummers have unloaded their wares from the train.*

*Interior of A. C. Elliott's Grocery, Johnston City, 1920s.
Behind the counter, from left to right, are Elliott, an unidentified employee, Billy Vick, and Erni Trinkle. Photo
courtesy of Mrs. Lorene Trout.*

Interior of W. R. Hodge General Merchandise, 908 South Court, Marion, around 1927. This store, open from 1920 to 1955, was later kown as Hodge's Grocery. Photo courtesy of Mrs. James W. Patterson.

Interior of Leming's Butcher Shop and Grocery, Main Street, West Frankfort, late 1920s. Shown are C. L. and Effie Crim Leming. Photo courtesy of Mrs. Lettie Hunter.

*Interior of the first Kroger store in Pinckneyville, late
1920s or early 1930s. At the extreme left is Lee Rice, the
manager, with Ernie Williams, the butcher, beside him.
At the far right is Resho Williams; second from right is
Gerald Opp. The others are unidentified. Photo courtesy
of Mrs. Opal Rice.*

Interior of Holmes Grocery and Meat Market, W. A. Broad Building, 304 West Main Street, Marion, 1920s. Left, Fred Holmes; right, Ebert Holmes. Photo courtesy of Charles D. Holmes.

Interior of Everett Fitzgerald's Grocery, 1503 East Main, West Frankfort, 1937. Shown is Everett Fitzgerald. Photo courtesy of Geneva Sinks.

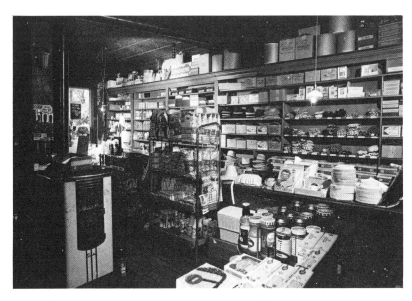

Interior of grocery at St. Libory, Illinois, about 1970. Photo courtesy of C. William Horrell.

Stout's General Merchandise, Gale, Illinois, about 1970.
Photo courtesy of C. William Horrell.

Clover Farm Store, Marissa, Illinois, 1985. Photo cour-
tesy of Tom Gorski.

Although I was very small, I have faint memories of the hustle and bustle, the clerks pointing out the different kinds of merchandise, the miners and their families choosing this and that.

This was my one, brief encounter with a company store. But it has stayed with me. For one reason, singers such as Tennessee Ernie Ford and Johnnie Cash have popularized Merle Travis' song, "Sixteen Tons":

> You load sixteen tons
> and what do you get?
> Another day older and deeper in debt.
> Saint Peter, don't you call me
> 'cause I can't go,
> I owe my soul to the company store.

Some did see the company stores as a means to squeeze every possible dollar out of the miners by advancing them credit against their wages, then charging exorbitant prices. This may have been true with some stores. But from what I've determined, the company stores in West Frankfort were there to keep a ready work force, more than anything else. They were open to the public, as well as miners, with prices only slightly above those in privately owned stores.

How did they help to keep a ready work force? Remember that the coal mines back then worked steadily in the winter months, poorly in the summers. Layoffs, strikes, and the like were common.

There was always the possibility that during the slack seasons some of the skilled miners would move to cities like Detroit in search of higher-paying jobs in the automobile plants. So by extending credit to its employees when work was slow, the coal companies were surer of keeping the men in southern Illinois.

The neighborhood grocery stores, which I've already described, were also known as "credit" stores, since most of them carried the miners when work was slow. But whereas a corner store might let a miner's bill run up as high as $300 to $400, the company stores could afford to go much higher, say $3,000 or more.

You can see, then, how a miner might "owe his soul to the company store" if he mismanaged his money or was forever spending his wages before he drew them.

Although Dad never worked in a shaft mine after I was four or five years old, I grew up hearing stories about the company stores as well as other aspects of mining. I picked this up while listening to Dad and his buddies reminisce about their old jobs.

Much of this I'd forgotten until I was researching this book and had a long talk with Peter Simko of West Frankfort, a miner for fifty-five years—from 1920 to 1975.

Peter Simko is a fascinating person, because his entire life is saturated with mine talk. His father, a native of Austria, emigrated to Montana in the 1880s to work in the mines there. When the railroads began to convert to diesels and the demand for Montana coal slowed down, the Simko family moved to West Frankfort. Pete was a boy at the time. As soon as he finished the eighth grade at the age of fourteen, he started to work in the mines around West Frankfort.

When the company learned how young Pete was, they laid him off. But he never washed his hands of coal dust. He got himself a horse and wagon and delivered coal until he was old enough to return to the mines.

Pete remembers the steam whistles, which were so characteristic of mine life until they phased out about 1925. "We lived by the mine whistles," Pete told me. "Set our clocks by them. Went to work by them. Mourned our dead by them."

The seven o'clock whistle was a signal for the employees to go below, riding down in the cage, then either walking or taking a man-trip on the underground rails to the various loading sites, which might be as much as a mile from where the main shaft entered the ground. Going down in the morning and coming up at night was on the workers' own time.

The eight o'clock whistle signaled the men to begin work. Since miners below might not hear the whistle, an electrician would blink the underground lights.

The twelve o'clock whistle announced lunch, when the miners opened their three-tiered aluminum buckets, with compartments for drinking water as well as sandwiches, cold fried chicken, raisin pie, and cornbread with sliced onions.

At four o'clock quitting time, if the whistle blew three long blasts, this meant the mine would work the next day. A single blast meant no work tomorrow. Pete told me that each mine had a whistle distinctive in pitch and direction. Thus, housewives knew before their men got home whether they'd be idle or working the next day.

One blast at any other time during the day meant the mine had "blown over," with no more work that day. The mine itself didn't "blow over" as in a windstorm; the expression meant there was no more work that day.

Or, if an explosion or cave-in killed a man, the engineer pulled the same "blow over" whistle. Imagine the apprehension of families when they heard a mine blow over, not knowing if it was just a breakdown or if one of their loved ones was hurt or dead. Pete knows what that means, for one day his family heard a mine blow over when his brother, John, was killed by a rockfall that broke his neck.

As we talked on, Pete told me about the job titles of the thirties. The mine manager was responsible for everything below and, at one time, did all the hiring. The top boss looked after things on the surface, including the washing, crushing, grading, and loading of the coal.

The average mine employed about five face bosses, one for each section underground where mining operations were underway. Each one bossed twelve to twenty men and was responsible for production. The mine superintendent was the boss of bosses. The mine examiners went down each morning to check roof conditions, gas, and general safety. No miners could go below until they pronounced conditions safe for work.

Hoisting engineers raised and lowered the cage which delivered the men below to work—and, throughout the day, raised the giant loads of coal. Other jobs were held by shot-firers, loaders, track layers, timekeepers, clerks, electricians, timbermen, storekeepers, trip riders, oilers, motormen, and the like.

To describe the mines themselves, the men used such words as face, bottom, top, tipple, hoist, cars and tracks, cage, washer, air shaft, fans, loading machines, cutting machine, washhouse, pump house, and the storehouse for dynamite.

The underground mines were not as safe as today. Landon Henderson of Marion, who retired with a fifty-year pin for working underground, started when the miners used grease lamps in which they burned lard oil. Then came carbide lamps, which fastened to the miners' caps with a clip. Landon says they poured water in the top section of these lamps, which in turn dripped to the bottom section filled with carbide. A lever made it possible to adjust the flow of water, creating the right amount of gas.

"At first, we lit our carbide lamps with matches," he told me as we munched on Brach's chocolate-covered cherries after one recent Christmas. "Then they came out with a small wheel which you spun with your thumb against a flint, which set off a spark. We furnished our own tools, lamps, and carbide. Dangerous work. No telling how many gas explosions those open-flame carbide lamps set off.

When I retired, we were using the safety lamps, powered by a battery that strapped on your back."

As Landon relived those days with me, he recalled how you could buy chickens on foot at some of the neighborhood stores. "Arthur Doerr had a store on East Boulevard near my home," Landon continued. "He kept a wire pen by the side of the store for chickens. You could buy one dressed out of the refrigerator, or he'd grab a live one for you, tie its legs together, stick its head through a hole in a paper sack, then let you carry it home to wring its neck in your own backyard."

At this point, Landon laughed as he recalled an incident from his boyhood in Tennessee. (One of the joys of listening to older persons are stories that come to them on the spur of the moment—experiences they hadn't thought of for years.)

"Before we moved to Illinois, I was always hearing about this fellow named Joe McClain," Landon began. "Joe was a restless fellow, never satisfied where he lived, always picking up and moving on. Seems that Joe owned a smart rooster that soon caught on. About once a week that rooster would come up to the house, roll over on his back, then stick his legs up in the air for Joe to tie. That sly rooster knew that on moving day, Joe would tie him up anyway and throw him in the wagon, so he just accomodated him real smart-like."

The coal-mining culture of southern Illinois as we knew it in the twenties and thirties is now gone, along with the carbide lamps, the company stores, and the steam whistles.

But men such as Pete Simko and Landon Henderson remember . . . and I remember, although most of my memories are faint echoes and mirrored reflections against the backdrop of Old West Mine and a trip to the Coal Fields Store.

BRILLIANTINE, COAL BUCKETS, AND TOOTSIE ROLLS

When I go in a store, I like to have a pretty good idea of what I want. And I don't believe in running from store to store, saving two cents here and there. Before you know it, you've burnt all you saved in gasoline. I have certain brands I stick with and I like to pay in cash. Lots of folks do buy on credit, but I don't if I can help it. When your Grandpa Gordon ran a store down in the country, he made a cardboard sign, lettered it himself in pencil, advising folks not to ask for credit.

But my mother and her dad were exceptions. In large numbers, miners depended on credit to survive layoffs. The neighborhood groceries of the thirties were commonly called "credit stores." Just as a big company store might carry a miner through an entire summer, the neighborhood stores would at least carry him from payday to payday.

In dredging up my own memories, I met all kinds of folks with recollections of little stores in southern Illinois that sold on credit. And I guess that was true nationwide.

Landon Henderson of Marion remembers some of the prosperous, pre-Depression days when corner stores would cash a miner's paycheck. "Course when I started in the mines, they paid in cash," Landon told me. "Some even paid in gold, before our government went off the gold standard. At one time, I had $3,000 saved up in gold coins. I didn't have to pick around then for bargains. One day I brought home a whole stalk of bananas—still green— hung it on the back porch and told my four kids to eat all they wanted."

The late Kate Throgmorton of Marion remembered when C. J. "Uncle Sid" Norman operated a general store right on the public square, where she bought eggs for ten cents a dozen. At one time, Mr. Norman was Sunday School superintendent at the First Baptist Church. He invited everyone who came in his store to attend. It came to be known as "Uncle Sid's Sunday School."

Louise Melcher Johns still talks about the Cross Roads Store, about six miles southeast of Vienna. "Many a bad winter day, my dad would saddle his horse and ride over to the Cross Roads Store to play checkers."

Joy Norris recalls the Mousser Store at Chamnestown south of Marion, and Violet Grisham tells of stories handed down about Ike Groves' store at the corner of the Williamson County fairgrounds in Marion. And Small's Food Store, still in business, has been at 1005 East Main in Marion for over a hundred years.

My wife, the former Bessie Emling who grew up on a farm south of Pinckneyville, glows with excitement when she describes a 1931 visit to the Matthews General Store.

"Matthews was then a little crossroads community nine miles southwest of Pinckneyville on the Illinois Central Railroad," she said. "Its general store included a post office where farmers could buy stamps and pick up their mail, general delivery. The same building doubled as a depot where you could buy a ticket and wait for the train, and also sell your milk, cream, and eggs.

"They'd candle the eggs, holding them up to a bright light, and test the cream with a Babcock tester. A chief joy of my mother and grandmother was to take their eggs there, along with live chickens in crates, to do their 'trading.'

"In the fall of 1931 when I entered the first grade at the nearby Matthews School, Mr. and Mrs. Henry Ahlers owned the store. Eva Ahlers Sullivan, their daughter, managed it while they farmed.

"Our teacher, Mae Dempsey Gunther, lived in Pinckneyville. But since parts of the road were deep in mud and ice during the winter, she boarded with the Ahlers, who lived in the back rooms of the store. The Ahlers also fixed her a noon sack lunch. On weekends, she went home to Pinckneyville.

"One afternoon when the roads were so bad that Dad couldn't come for me, I spent the night in the store—the rooms in the back, that is. It was a heavenly dream. Most of all because, when morning came, Mrs. Ahlers fixed me the same lunch as she did for Miss Dempsey. Imagine a first grader, opening her lunch at noon and eating exactly what the teacher had!

"I can still see that lunch, which consisted of three kinds of food I'd never tasted. Actually, Mrs. Ahlers had fixed it the night before. I watched with amazement as she took boiling water and mixed the first gelatin I'd ever seen. It smelled terrible at the time, but I loved it. She poured the warm gelatin into individual aluminum molds, apparently made for that purpose. I took my little tin of gelatin to school the next day, along with a spoon. It was plain—no fruit.

"Then she made a sandwich of the first bakery bread I recall seeing, plus my first commercial lunch meat. Growing up on a farm where we were almost self-sufficient in the thirties, we just didn't buy delicacies such as bologna and bakery bread.

"Today, there's no post office at Matthews, no depot, no general store, no school. All that's left are my memories. But to me, they're as real as the winter day in 1931–32 when I tasted those first store-bought delicacies.

"Oh, yes, the Matthews Baptist Church is still there and I treasure its heritage. The sandwich bread I enjoyed in 1931 is long since gone, but the Bread of Life I found in that church still nourishes me."

Now, would you like to tiptoe inside a neighborhood

store of that era? We can, with a little imagination.

To do so, let's drive back up to West Frankfort and talk with Ed Migielicz, whose parents owned a store there for forty years. Ed's basement is crammed with some of the original furnishings, including the old cash register and the long, massive counter.

Jacob Migielicz Groceries and Meats was open for forty years, from about 1920 to 1960, at 2101 East Elm in West Frankfort. Long-time resident Pete Simko remembers the Migielicz store well. "I knew their son, Ed, when he was in diapers," he grinned at me.

Ed's parents were born in the Ukraine. Both emigrated to the States when they were seventeen, then met and were married in Illinois. Jacob finished the fourth grade, but Ed's mother had no schooling. Although she never learned to read or write, she presided for forty years at that big, brass cash register which her son, Ed, now treasures.

"My parents had a large credit business," Ed recalls. "Mother never wanted a customer to know she couldn't read. So she learned to memorize as many as three or four grocery lists at a time. Then when I came in, she'd dictate the purchases and prices to me, while I entered them in the customer's credit (or sales) book."

Both parents spoke Ukrainian as well as English. Mr. Migielicz could also understand customers who spoke Bulgarian, Hungarian, Lithuanian, Italian, German, and Polish. This was important, for many nationalities were represented in such coal towns as West Frankfort, Ziegler, Herrin, and Christopher.

A massive wooden counter dominated the store, one with twenty-three glass-front bins. Depending on a customer's order, the storekeeper opened the proper bin from the back and scooped out so many pounds. A sample of the contents in each of the twenty-three could be seen through the glass fronts. Thus, if a housewife couldn't speak English or didn't know the proper name for a product, she could point, say, to the dried shelled peas behind the glass front.

The Migielicz family lived in three rooms at the side of their store. As many as twelve hundred miners a day passed by on foot when Old Ben No. 9 was working and before cars were common.

To accommodate the miners who often stopped to buy "fixins" for their buckets, they opened at 5:00 A.M. and didn't close until 10:00 P.M.! At night, miners loafed by the big round heating stove, sitting on benches provided for them. Here you could learn just about anything you wanted to know about coal mining, much of it from the lips of emigrants who barely spoke English.

When the miners were out of work or fell on hard times, Mr. Migielicz carried them on credit. He helped many of them get their citizenship papers. Occasionally, he'd loan a miner "two dollars until payday."

The typical miner wore bib overalls, denim shirts, denim jackets, and metal-toed shoes, all of which Mr. Migielicz stocked. He carried Arnold's line of overalls, but if a miner preferred Osh Kosh B'Gosh, he went to J. V. Walker & Co.

Migielicz also sold aluminum dinner buckets, miners' caps, carbide lamps and the carbide to fuel them, picks, shovels, axes, work gloves, heavy woolen socks, and long underwear.

Ed recalls the hard work his parents put into their store: "For one thing, they made some of the products we sold. We raised chickens and hogs right there in town and butchered them for sale in the store. Other times we'd buy a beef and butcher it. Mother could dress a chicken for a customer or sell it on foot, tying its legs together and sticking its head through a hole in a paper sack.

"We made and sold our own smoked sausage, especially at Christmas and Easter, plus homemade dill pickles and kraut, which we stored in big glass jars. Ourselves, we ate lots of stew and soup made from leftover bones. Steaks and pork chops were to sell, not to eat.

"Dad bought bacon by the case in big slabs, then cut it into smaller slabs—kept better that way, rather than sliced. In the backyard, we kept a sandstone rotary operated with foot pedals, on which once a week Dad sharpened all his butcher knives, while a stream of water played on the stone. Inside, he used a 'steel' for in-between sharpenings, to take the rough edges off the knives. A flat emery stone on the counter served the same purpose."

What were some products you were likely to see in Jacob Migielicz's store—or any store of that era?

Lots of items were sold in bulk, such as rice, potatoes, coffee, sugar, flour, ground pepper, pinto beans, prunes, navy beans, dried apricots and peaches, Great Northern beans, raisins, butter beans, and dried green peas.

Also soda crackers, candy, rolled oats, pickles (in kegs), shredded coconut, salt, meal, cookies, flaked hominy, lard (in metal cans), carbide (in twenty-five or fifty pound metal cans), plus chicken feed, such as shelled or cracked corn, cracked wheat, or mixed grains.

Mrs. Dilla Hall of Marion can never forget the taste of flaked hominy, which she can't find in the stores today. "My, it was good for breakfast, came shredded like coconut," she told me.

"Bulk" means these products came in big sacks, bins, kegs, jugs, or boxes, and the storekeeper weighed up however much you wanted. A customer who asked for a "poke of coffee" meant a pound of coffee in a paper sack. A "poke of sugar" meant the same.

Coffee was ground to order in a hand-cranked mill. Or some stores sold "green" coffee, just like it was picked.

That way, you could take it home and roast it to taste—light or dark—in the oven of a coal or wood-burning cookstove.

If you wanted a soft drink, you didn't buy a six-bottle carton or a case. Usually it was a bottle at a time, which you opened and drank right there.

Whole red peppers were strung and suspended from the same ceiling where hung stalks of bananas. Kerosene (coal oil) was hand-pumped from a big tank that might stand out on the porch. Vinegar came in fifty-five gallon barrels, each with its own wooden pump, a popular item around home-canning time when housewives made their own pickles and the like.

Customers also bought most of their candy in bulk: red and black licorice, hoarhound, peanut brittle, Tootsie rolls, chocolate cherries (at Christmas), lemon gum drops, orange slices, candy corn, and tiny wax bottles filled with sweet syrup.

Also chocolate-covered peanuts, malted milk balls, suckers, red hots, peanut butter bars, coconut marshmallows, kisses, caramels and, near Valentine's Day, candied hearts with such mottoes as "Watch my dust," as well as jawbreakers in a variety of colors—red, purple, green, and blue.

And it was taken for granted that whenever a customer paid his back bill, the storekeeper threw in a free sack of candy for the kids.

If you were a miner and used tobacco, you could find plug or chewing tobacco, which was permitted below ground. The Migielicz store stocked plug tobacco such as Day's Work or Mule in big slabs, then sliced it into smaller pieces with a tobacco cutter and sacked it. Customers who rolled their own could buy Bull Durham or Golden Grain in cotton sacks with little drawstrings, including cigarette papers, for five cents a bag.

For home remedies, you could buy Kim's castor oil, St. Joseph Diuretic pills, Vick's Salve, Hunt's Lightening Oil liniment ("good for man or beast"), H & R cough syrup (made with pine tar and honey), Rucker's Triena (laxative for children), and Black-Draught ("a purely vegetable laxative").

If you still lit your home with lamps, how about a new kerosene lamp, or maybe just a wick and burner, or a new glass chimney? And don't forget washtubs and rubbing boards, ash shovels for cleaning out the heating stove, coal buckets, Ball glass jars, rubbers, and lids, stove polish, stovepipe, threads of all kinds plus buttons, ribbons, and bolts of dry goods.

Bessie, my wife, remembers when sugar and flour were first packaged in ten- and twenty-pound cotton sacks. The sacks featured printed patterns in color, such as flowers and geometric designs. "Housewives cut up these sacks and made aprons, curtains, dishtowels, quilt pieces, house dresses, and even Sunday-school dresses," she said.

"Some of the sacks came just the right size for pillow cases, and a mother felt lucky if she found three or four bags with the same pattern. Or, a larger woman might need six or eight sacks for her dress. Neighbors would save these sacks and trade around to get matching patterns.

"My mother, who bought in big quantities, had a way of sniffing out identical patterns. How happy it made her when she didn't have to buy the material for a new dress, but salvaged enough in her own kitchen after emptying the sugar and flour sacks."

As more homes bought washing machines, new kinds of soap powders came on the market. Manuel Strachan, who owned the Neighborhood Market at 305 East Warder in Marion, remembers when most soap was sold in bars, which was best for rubbing clothes by hand.

"We sold the big yellow bars of laundry soap, ten bars to a sack or wrapped in butcher paper," he told me. "Next came soap flakes such as Fels Naptha and Lux. Duz was the first soap powder I remember selling, followed by Rinso and Oxydol. But the first boxes were so tiny, compared with today's giant family sizes."

"Back then, customers would ask the clerk in a little store like mine to do anything. I remember one family who always wanted round steak cut a special way—chopped into small pieces, which they claimed they ate raw. How, I don't know. And we sold mostly white bread. Oh, once in a while a bakery would bring a rye or a wheat bread. I remember the first sliced loaves, made by Wonder Bread. Until then, every housewife owned a bread knife. And bread had more texture then, like homemade. Today it's all fluffed up, lots of air in it. You can mash it with your hand and almost make dough out of it again."

How about a bottle of Brilliantine to slick back your teenage son's hair? Or a bottle of rose water for your complexion? Or a pair of Stick-'Em-On soles for those holes about to break through the bottoms of your shoes? Or a bottle of Little Boy Blue bluing to whiten your wash?

But wait, this is not an encyclopedia. So let's stop where we are, pick up our sack of groceries, go home, and listen to Lowell Thomas and the news, Amos 'n Andy, Little Orphan Annie, Lum and Abner, Jack Armstrong the All-American Boy, The Lone Ranger, Inner Sanctum, The Shadow, Boston Blackie, or Fibber McGee and Molly.

We could tune in a little music and listen to Smilin' Ed McConnell or Lula Bell and Scotty. Or maybe hear Kate Smith sing, "When the Moon Comes Over the Mountain," then send in for her free cookbook from the Calumet Baking Company—which tells you how to use all those new products showing up every day now on Mr. Migielicz's shelves in West Frankfort.

THE STREET MERCHANT GO-GETTERS

*I didn't fix any dessert for supper, so take this nickel and
go out and watch for Bennie's ice-cream wagon. It's
about time for him. Sit on the curb and wait until he's
even with the house before you go in the street. It's getting dark and the cars might not see you.*

One of my earliest memories in Marion is the tinkling
bell, usually at dusk, of Bennie the ice-cream man. Ben
Mazzara and his wife were emigrants from Sicily, and I
admired this short, black-haired man for making his own
job when few were to be found.

In the summertime, he drove a little white, enclosed
wagon around the streets, peddling ice-cream cups, popsicles, Wonder bars, and other frozen novelties. A pony
pulled the cart-like wagon. Mr. Mazzara sat up front, then
reached around in the back for his ice cream when he had
a customer.

North State Street, where I lived, must have been near
the end of his route, for I remember him coming around
about dusk. As the late summer days shortened, dark
might catch him and he would urge his pony along at a
faster clip.

I suppose all of us have tucked away in our memories
an ice cream man of some sort. This one is special to me
not only for the sweet, drippy popsicles he sold me, but
that he was an entrepeneur. While you could buy ice
cream and soft drinks in any neighborhood store, here
was a go-getter who put his little store on wheels. I think
of him as a "storekeeper" during the thirties as much as
J. C. Swan, Lon Norman, or Herman Garrison.

When the weather turned cold in the fall, Bennie parked
his wagon in a shed and peddled hot tamales on foot, up
and down the streets of downtown Marion.

The whole family pitched in to make the tamales, which soon won a reputation for their succulent goodness. Bennie must have toted that little gas-fired, portable oven a hundred thousand miles crying, "Hot tamales! Hot tamales! Get your tamales while they're hot."

His tamales sold briskly on cold nights following high-school football and basketball games. Many of the fans walked home through the crisp night and the pungent tamales were a treat.

When Ben met a customer, he set the oven down on the sidewalk, opened the lid, and with a proud flourish served the tamales wrapped in genuine cornhusks. Steam from the oven swished around his eager customers, while a streetlight cast a warm glow on the scene that made you think of a Charles Dickens etching from your high school English literature book.

Since Mr. Mazzara was a short man, the oven seemed to graze the sidewalk as he made his way to another cluster of buyers. The way he shifted the oven from one hand to another, occasionally setting it down to rest, made me think it got pretty heavy after several hours of walking around the public square, up North Market, and out West Main toward the high school.

The Mazzaras had two daughters and a son named Tony, a short, fat, curly-haired boy who looked a lot like his dad. Tony wanted to play in the grade-school band, but his parents couldn't afford a new instrument on the income from tamales and ice-cream bars.

So Mr. Mazzara bred Lady, the pony that pulled his cart, and one Sunday she gave birth to a little colt. "We named her Sunday, for the day of the week she was born," their daughter Mary told me. "Then Daddy sold Sunday, and that's how we paid for an E-flat clarinet for Tony."

It was a good investment, for when Tony grew up, he taught music for thirty-two years in the public schools.

During the last twenty of those years, he was unit band director for the Rochester school district, near Springfield, Illinois.

As soon as Tony was big enough to carry an oven, Ben put him on the streets selling tamales, too. Tony's little arms were so short that he sometimes banged the bottom of his oven against a curb.

"Daddy insisted on wrapping his tamales in real corn shucks, rather than the parchment paper that most businesses use," Mary told me. "Each fall, Daddy would find a farmer who agreed to give us husks from his corn in exchange for picking it. On weekends, all of us went to his fields and carefully stripped the rows clean, leaving not a single ear.

"Next we carried the corn into the barn where we shucked it. We were well-organized. First, us kids would hand the ears, one by one, to Daddy. He sat on a bench in front of a homemade circular blade that he had rigged up. He held the ears, one by one, up to the blade that cut the shucks off clean. We sang and told stories while we worked.

"Back home, we picked the silks from the shucks, which always left you sticky and itching. Tony and I usually argued over who would get in the bathtub first, we were itching so badly."

Mrs. Mazzara then made the tamales in her kitchen, carefully wrapping each in a southern Illinois corn shuck, which had been sterilized in boiling water.

We sometimes think that because someone's in business, the money comes easy. Not necessarily so. I think of Jacob Migielicz's family in West Frankfort, selling roasts and sausages over the counter, but eating stews and soups themselves, made from leftover bones.

Tony once told me, in a reflective mood, how this was true with his family: "Each Sunday, my two sisters and I shared one Pepsi-Cola for dinner. We measured it carefully in three glasses, making sure each got his share. But twice a year, we really splurged. On Christmas and New Year's, Momma gave us all the ravioli we could hold, and each of us got his own full bottle of Pepsi!"

Today, when many youngsters go to the family refrigerator and pour a soft drink as casually as Tony and I reached for a dipper of drinking water in the thirties, we find it hard to believe his story about the full Pepsi only twice a year.

On another occasion Tony remarked to me, "Bob, there's one thing I'd like before I die. I want to be retired for just one year and sit on my front porch in Rochester in September and watch the kids go off to school, knowing I have no responsibility."

That wish didn't come true, and I'm not all that sure it would have pleased him, anyway. For you see, Tony was a product of the Depression, the offspring of a hard-working family.

When I think of Ben, wearing blisters on his hands, toting that tamale oven; or my cousin Erby Hastings knocking on doors for grocery orders at 5:00 A.M.; or Ed Migielicz's mother memorizing those grocery orders lest her customers catch on that she couldn't write; or Lizzie Davis saving a few pennies ordering pork and beans by the case at Sears; or Dad sleeping in his store to keep it open while the family was quarantined—it's then that I think of an eight-letter, hyphenated word.

It's spelled go-getter. Folks had to be go-getters in the thirties, especially if they had few job skills and could draw only on their own self-determination.

I say all this to say that Tony, at heart, was a go-getter. And his kind doesn't really enjoy sitting on the sidelines, watching the world go by. They've got to be part of it— shuckin' that corn, stuffin' those tamales, totin' that oven.

WHAT! SHOP WITH A BABY BUGGY?

Lizzie, I'll tell you what's a fact, no one's going to make me go in there and push one of those baby buggies around. I wouldn't know where to look for nothing, sashaying up and down the aisles.

Ruby, I'm the same way. If that new Kroger wants my business, they'll wait on me like they always have. Things are getting too modern around here to suit the likes of me and you.

During the thirties, a businessman by the name of Sylvan N. Goldman owned two struggling grocery chains in Oklahoma. Goldman noted that customers stopped buying when their baskets got too heavy to carry. He experimented by mounting baskets on wheels. By doing so, Mr. Goldman set off a retailing revolution. Today, self-service supermarkets with their rows and rows of shiny pushcarts are as common as layoffs were in the Great Depression.

The long arm of self-service retailing reached my hometown of Marion in the fall of 1941. I know. I was there.

One afternoon, on my way home from high school, I noticed a new building going up at 507 West Main. It was a long, low, squat brick building with big plate glass windows all across the front. What looked like a huge parking lot was being paved next door.

A sign in front announced the exciting news—Marion's first self-service supermarket. And wonder of wonders! Customers would wait on themselves rather than stepping up to a counter and asking for items one by one, while harried clerks traced and retraced their steps, sometimes bumping into each other and dropping canned goods that rolled into dark corners.

Customers would load their groceries into shopping

carts—quickly labeled "baby buggies" by Mom and her neighbor, Lizzie Davis—then push them through one of several check-out counters. Although this is common today, you must imagine yourself in the thirties to appreciate how revolutionary it was.

For a year, I'd been working two afternoons a week, sweeping out the Sears retail order office on North Market and washing its front windows. I didn't like the job because the other workers were older, and, when I swept out the back room, I had to move every one of the mail-order packages, sweep, then move them all back again.

So I applied for a job at the new Kroger before the building was completed. Kroger officials had already named Harl Browning as the manager, since he had long experience at their earlier outlets on North Market and East Main.

The talk was that if anyone could make a go of the new supermarket, Harl Browning could. A friendly, outgoing man with a ready smile, he was also a leader in the First Baptist Church.

Mr. Browning hired me about the same time he employed such friends of mine as Raymond Allen, Johnnie Wolff, J. C. Mitchell, Art "Boots" Bauer, Vernell McAlpin, and Ralph Sims. He hired us as stock boys, except Sims, who managed the produce department. This meant we did anything Mr. Browning wanted done: unloading delivery trucks, stocking shelves, sacking orders and carrying them to the cars, sweeping, mopping, washing windows, cleaning toilets, trimming produce, running errands, or whatever.

It was a fun place to work—after school, Saturdays, and full time during the summer months. We also helped stock shelves before opening day.

At last, all was ready—shelves crammed until they

groaned under the weight of thousands of cans of fruits and vegetables, the long meat counter across the back, the gleaming produce case with its freshly sprinkled lettuce and carrots and cabbage and radishes, the long line of shiny new carts that seemed to stretch at least a mile, like a freight train ready to pull out of the section yards, two or three cash registers that responded with lightning speed to even the fastest cashier, plus stacks and stacks of bags and empty boxes beside the check-out counters, waiting to be filled with the first groceries ever bought in Marion at a real supermarket!

Were Marion a great seacoast city and a battleship about to be launched, the day could have held no more excitement for me. And, although Mom and Lizzie Davis swore they'd never be caught pushing baby buggies in a grocery store, I'll let you guess who were some of the first customers!

What we didn't realize was that we were standing on the dividing line between the friendly days of the neighborhood stores and the more efficient but less personal supermarkets.

Although one still sees an occasional neighborhood shop, plus the popular twenty-four-hour-a-day convenience stores, most of the Mom and Pop stores are probably gone for good.

Looking back, I see how Harl Browning helped bridge that transition in our community. He kept close to the front doors, especially on Saturdays when crowds were big, speaking to every possible customer. He combined old-fashioned friendliness with fast check-out lanes, giving his customers a little of that old-time nostalgia.

World War II was approaching and it too served as a transitional wedge, putting the slower-paced twenties and thirties into the mothballs of yesterday's scrapbooks.

Anticipating wartime shortages, Mr. Browning ordered a whole trailer-load of canned salmon. We stored case after case to the ceiling of the stockroom, passing them up hand over hand, row after row after row, until it seemed we had every salmon ever caught by man stored away for our customers. I can see the arched backs of the red salmons pictured on the cans and hear Mr. Browning say, "There probably won't be any more." And there wasn't, not until the war ended in 1945.

Although we had to do our work right—such as carefully packaging each sack so that cans went on the bottom with bread and perishables on top, even if it was only one small sack—we had lots of good times.

Raymond Allen remembers more than I do—such as the time Mr. Browning gave him and Vernell McAlpin a dressing down for throwing eggs at the picket signs of union organizers. And locking Johnnie Wolff in the walk-in cooler amd removing the handle, to which Johnnie responded by calmly sitting down in his frigid prison and helping himself to the big California grapes. And the day Mr. Browning fired J. C. Mitchell when he found him lying atop a stack of toilet tissue, eating bananas and reading comic books. And butcher Bob Short chasing Raymond with a meat cleaver for teasing him—the "chase" ending unexpectedly when Raymond ran into a thousand-can display of split peas, knocking down in seconds what he'd worked on for hours.

Like Browning, R. W. "Bob" Short was a deacon in the First Baptist Church. A big, likeable fellow who knew most of his customers by their first names, Bob was the only butcher I knew who could cut any piece of meat to order while carrying on a 500-word-a-minute conversation.

Invariably, Bob began each working day by reciting, so everyone could hear, the jingle:

> Another day,
> Another dollar.
> A million days,
> A millionaire.

Although this was a new supermarket, meat was still custom-cut. No antiseptic, pre-cut, plastic-wrapped meat in Bob's refrigerator. Oh, he may have pre-ground the hamburger, but he still liked to pull a pork loin out of the meat case, lean way over so the customer could get a good look, then ask, "Now Ruby, how about six thick chops right out of the center—money can't buy you no better, I don't care if you go to A & P or the moon."

Best of all, I remember Deacon Short's public prayers at church. I memorized exactly how he would start: "Lord, we want to thank you that everything's as well with us as it is." As a boy, I tended to discount this part of his prayer, wondering if it weren't more appropriate to ask God to make things better. But with the mellowing of the years, I've come to see Bob's wisdom.

I often wondered if that prayer was original or if he'd picked it up somewhere. In later years, I often heard my father-in-law, Herman Emling, use the same words. Herman once served as pastor of the Holt's Prairie Baptist Church, a rural congregation between Pinckneyville and DuQuoin, Illinois. Bob Short had relatives in that area.

Did Bob hear it from Herman, or Herman from Bob? Or did each hear it from a third source? Did some saint of God, maybe in the last century, originate that expression? Was it then copied by generation after generation?

It doesn't matter. What matters is whether you and I can find something in every day to be thankful for, regardless of how bleak the outlook.

What did we teenagers earn at the new supermarket? Raymond says we were paid $18.75 a week the summer we worked full time. "Full time" meant six days a week, about ten hours a day. Except Saturdays when we started at 7:00 A.M. and closed at 8:00 P.M., followed by however long it took to sweep and mop the entire store, pack the leftover produce in the cooler, wash the meat counter, and get our pay.

On those long days, Bob Short often stood on a soft drink case to ease his feet on the hard floor, and the better to see the milling customers in front of him.

Mr. Browning paid us off in cash. After the doors were locked and he had cleared the cash registers and while we were mopping, he'd call us one by one up to the front check-out counter, much like a country schoolteacher of past generations might pass out treats on Friday afternoons to winners in the spelling bee.

By the end of the summer, I had $100 put away in postal savings (still didn't trust those banks too much!). I don't think I made $18.75 a week that summer. If so, I'd have saved more than $100, for I seldom spent anything, so intent was I on going to school. Maybe Raymond was worth more.

Each noon, I pedaled my bicycle home for lunch. On Saturdays, we also got a supper break, but only for a few minutes. To save time, I ate supper at my Aunt Bertha Anderson's, who lived closer to the store. But Aunt Bertha, who was conditioned as a miner's wife to breakfast at 5:00 A.M. and supper at 4:30 P.M. (earlier if possible!), was not about to wait for me until 5:30 or 6:00. So all that summer, on Saturdays, she saved me back a big slab of her golden yellow cornbread, which she baked every day of the world in her massive, black cookstove. As I left the store, I reached in the dairy case for a pint of homogenized milk.

The cold cornbread and sweet milk reminded me of how, during the Depression, I had stood in line at the Marion

City Dairy on Saturday mornings, an enamel water bucket in my hand, waiting my turn to buy a nickel's worth of skim milk. But I could afford whole milk now, and I savored every drop.

Somehow, I was never anxious for the store to close. I paid little attention to the long hours. I liked the camaraderie, the fun, the joking, the racing with my peers to see who could bag his groceries fastest, run them out to a car, then back again to grab another open sack.

When the last mop was wrung out and the last carrot put in the cooler for the weekend, I rode home in the dark. Usually, Mom and Dad were in bed unless it was an extra hot night and they were sitting up until the bedrooms cooled off.

By then we had an indoor bathroom, but no hot water. "Bob, the teakettle's full and sitting on the stove. Light the gas and get your bath water real hot, but don't let it boil over."

I poured the steaming water in the tub, turned on the cold water to temper it, pulled off my work clothes, then soaked away the tiredness of another fourteen-hour day.

Before going to bed I reached for my box of church envelopes and put aside a tithe of what I'd made for Sunday school the next day. The rest of it, I folded in my wallet and laid on the dresser.

I was a very rich teenage boy, all made possible by Mr. Goldman's baby-buggy shopping carts.

RELISH THE MOMENT

You couldn't pay me to live in a city like St. Louis or Chicago. I've lived in Marion since I was a little girl, just twelve miles from where I was born. And Eldon, he grew

up out near Paulton, only six miles from here. I can go to
St. Louis for two or three days, but when I cross that
Eads Bridge into Illinois, I feel like I'm in God's country
again. There's no pleasure in the world like coming back
home, sleeping in your own bed, eating from your own
table.

Not everyone can live in a small town, as my parents
did. In fact, most people don't. Millions prefer the business and industry, cultural advantages, job opportunities,
parks, prestigious universities, theaters, zoos, research
hospitals, sports stadiums, giant air terminals, the excitement and homogeneity of big cities.

No Herculean power could take such cities as Los An-
geles, Houston, New York, London, Paris, Berlin, Rome,
Moscow, Peking, Hong Kong, Bombay, Mexico City, Buenos
Aires, and Rio de Janeiro and disperse them into neat
little towns where all the kids walk to school, friendly
shopkeepers know you by name, and six cars can tie up
traffic at an intersection.

And with the growth of cities and the interstate highways have come the shopping malls and giant grocery
chains that stock thousands of items, compared with
the hundreds you might buy in the thirties. Farm and village folk think nothing of driving fifty miles to the near-
est mall.

Much of this is good. There's no way we can go back to
the family-oriented stores and find the quantity and variety of food we enjoy today.

Yet there lingers in each of us a yearning for neighborhood, that feeling of belonging, of home, of roots, of the
familiar. We fear the swollen river of humanity lest it
sweep us downstream over a Niagara of anonymity. We
dread the day when there's no one left to call us by our
first name.

That's why, fifty years later, I sometimes close my eyes
and imagine I'm eleven years old again. The summertime
streets of Marion are quiet, broken only by the occasional
shout of a paper-boy, pushing his one-wheel news cart
down North State Street.

It's a Sunday. And, whether or not my parents attend,
my mother remembers the vow she made when I was
born, that I'd be a regular in Sunday school.

At 8:45, I leave the house, Bible and Sunday-school
booklet in hand, for the First Baptist Church downtown.

I pass Swan's Store. The door's closed, the little single-
bulb lights switched off, the baskets of corn and green
beans moved inside from the porch. This day is different.
It's for more than buying and selling.

If the creek's not too high and I can jump it without
muddying my Sunday shoes, I take the shortcut through
Mr. Swan's empty lot. If not, I continue down East De-
Young to North Market, past the home of city school superintendent H. O. Belford who, had he chosen and if I'd
sat still, could have sneaked me into the first grade when
I was five.

As I pass the Davis Motor Company on North Market
and take a quick look at the new Fords on display, the
nine o'clock Methodist bell begins to ring. You can hear it
for blocks.

I turn right at West White and in half a minute bound
up the steps to my aunt and uncle's home, the Andersons.
Bertha's whistling a tune, maybe a hymn, as she beats the
meringue for two lemon pies. Charley's shaving.

"How's your mother and dad? You sure are dressed up
this morning. Is that a new shirt?"

Across the street, the high-pitched whine of the cutting
and polishing machines of Thurmond Monument Company are silent. This is Sunday, and it's different.

Knowing the 9:30 starting bell at the First Methodist

Church will ring any minute now, I hurry the rest of the way to church, crossing the Illinois Central tracks and glancing left at the big pillars of the red brick railroad station.

Jewel Bethel, a school janitor, is our teacher. "Boys," he begins, "let's open to Luke 12:15 and see what it says: 'Take heed, and beware of covetousness: for a man's life consisteth not in the abundance of the things which he possesseth.'"

"Good," he continues, "now turn back to Matthew 6:25–34: 'Take no thought for your life, what ye shall eat, or what ye shall drink; nor yet what for your body, what ye shall put on . . . your heavenly Father knoweth that ye have need of all these things . . . Sufficient unto the day is the evil thereof.'"

The lesson is simple but profound: Life is more than what you eat and wear. I realize my boyhood memoirs are idyllic, that when I open my eyes, things are not what they were in 1935, nor do I want all of them to be. But Mr. Bethel's lesson still jumps out at me—life is something deep and hidden, warm and touching, divorced from dollar signs and wed to simplicity.

Among other things, we have lost the casualness of small town and rural life, the finding of fun in simple pursuits. Neighbors have turned into competitors as we race to see who gets the best parking spaces at the supermarket.

We seldom walk anywhere to shop, as we once did. And when we do jump in the car to go shopping, it may as likely be eleven o'clock at night or a Sunday afternoon.

The quiet, tree-lined streets and quaint, downtown business districts are no longer at the center of community life. Shopping malls are usually off to one side, not in the center. Main Street is no longer the main street. The marketplace is on the periphery, yet its products have monopolized the center of our affections.

Days and nights and weekends and months and years and faces and holidays and brand names and generic names and computerized check-out counters and credit cards and Sundays and competitiveness and consumerism and obesity and sleeplessness and anxiety are all run together—forming one big, glittering, non-stop, pulsating, herky-jerky neon billboard of life like those you see at the casinos in Las Vegas and Reno.

We ask ourselves, "Will the pace ever slacken? Will barefoot kids ever again push open screen doors at corner grocers and set the bells a-ringing?"

The answer, of course, is No. We cannot go back to yesterday. But we can make the most of today. It was 1980 before I wrote the following essay, putting into words the feelings that germinated during my boyhood in Marion, Illinois:

The Station *

Tucked away in our subconscious minds is an idyllic vision in which we see ourselves on a long journey that spans an entire continent. We're traveling by train and, from the windows, we drink in the passing scenes of cars on nearby highways, of children waving at crossings, of cattle grazing in distant pastures, of smoke pouring from power plants, of row upon row upon row of cotton and corn and wheat, of flatlands and valleys, of city skylines and village halls.

But uppermost in our conscious minds is our final destination—for at a certain hour and on a given day, our train will finally pull into the station with bells ringing, flags waving, and bands playing. And once that day comes, so many wonderful dreams will come true. So restlessly, we pace the aisles and count the

* Adapted from an editorial in January 2, 1980 issue of *The Illinois Baptist*. Used here by permission.

miles, peering ahead, waiting, waiting, waiting for the station.

"Yes, when we reach the station, that will be it!" we promise ourselves. "When we're eighteen . . . win that promotion . . . put the last kid through college . . . buy that 450 SL Mercedes Benz . . . pay off the mortgage . . . have a nest egg for retirement."

From that day on, we will all live happily ever after.

Sooner or later, however, we must realize there is no station in this life, no one earthly place to arrive at once and for all. The journey is the joy. The station is an illusion—it constantly outdistances us. Yesterday's a memory, tomorrow's a dream. Yesterday belongs to a history, tomorrow belongs to God. Yesterday's a fading sunset, tomorrow's a faint sunrise. Only today is there light enough to love and live.

So, gently close the door on yesterday and throw the key away. It isn't the burdens of today that drive men mad, but rather the regret over yesterday and the fear of tomorrow.

"Relish the moment" is a good motto, especially when coupled with Psalm 118:24, "This is the day which the Lord hath made; we will rejoice and be glad in it."

So stop pacing the aisles and counting the miles. Instead, swim more rivers, climb more mountains, kiss more babies, count more stars. Laugh more and cry less. Go barefoot oftener. Eat more ice cream. Ride more merry-go-rounds. Watch more sunsets. Life must be lived as we go along.

GOOD NIGHT, SWEET PRINCE

Son, when you go down to the funeral home this morning, take these two pair of long underwear. Tell Mr.

Mitchell to put both pairs on Eldon. He was so thin when he died. This will help fill him out, make his suit fit better.

The last thing I did for Dad was to go to Albright's Men's Store on the public square, known for years as "Powell's Best Clothes in Egypt." (Southern Illinois is commonly referred to as Little Egypt.) We'd decided to bury him in an older gray suit that had always looked good on him, but he needed a new white shirt.

Being a veteran of the Great Depression, he would have been pleased to know I found an all-cotton Manhattan dress shirt, one of the best, on sale for half price.

Mom, the person in our family who seemed to think of everything, came up with the idea of two pair of union suits "to fill him out so he'll look better."

As I walked out North Market to the Mitchell Funeral Home, the shirt and underwear under my arm, the words of William Shakespeare surrounded me:

Now cracks a noble heart. Good-night, sweet prince, and flights of angels sing thee to thy rest!
                                        Hamlet, Act V, Scene 2

On that May morning of 1968, I relived my fascination with neighborhood stores, an interest that began with the first stories I heard about my Grandpa Gordon's stores.

And then there had been the Smith and Hepler Store where my brother, LaVerne, worked a few months as a teenager. How prosperous and grown-up he seemed to me at the time. He even had a girlfriend and, at Christmas, he ordered her a stunning blue dresser set from Spiegel May-Sterns in Chicago. When the set arrived, we crowded around it while he opened it.

Mom thought it was so pretty. She held it up to the light,

turned it over, looked in the mirror, watched it glitter and reflect against the wall. Like any housewife of her day with long hair, Mom owned assorted combs and brushes. But never a matching set that came by parcel post from Chicago!

And then I thought of Dad and the two stores he had owned, although he was no great success as a merchant. With limited education and no job skills other than mining, he had to make the most of his jobs. "I'll try anything once," he often claimed.

If Dad set no records as a storekeeper, another Illinoisan didn't do too well himself. I'm thinking about Abraham Lincoln who, as a boy in Indiana, entertained with his storytelling the men who loafed around the general store in the crossroads village of Gentryville.

When Lincoln moved to the tiny village of New Salem, twenty miles northwest of Springfield, Illinois, Denton Offutt gave him a job clerking in his store. Lincoln earned little in wages, but he did benefit by being allowed to sleep in a room back of the store. However, the business failed within a few months and the store closed.

Toward the end of the Depression, Dad tried to sell merchandise door to door for the L. B. Price Mercantile Company. But money was still tight and his sales were sluggish. In later years, Dad sold W. T. Raleigh products, one of his more successful ventures. He cultivated a large number of regular customers, all over town. Many of these were older persons who welcomed his knock at the door. They knew he'd come inside, sit down and visit, whether they bought anything or not.

He lent a sympathetic ear to the problems of the aging—their pension checks were stretching too thin, their rheumatism was keeping them awake at nights, the water heater spluttered and died and they worried what it would cost to hire a plumber to come out and patch it up, and on and on. "I know what you mean, I know how you feel," he often replied. And to some, that was worth more than gold.

By now I had reached the funeral home. "Tell your mother I'll be glad to use both pairs when I get him dressed," Mr. Mitchell said.

And Mr. Mitchell did. And Dad's frail body looked better. Silent now were the mine whistles . . . ended were the payless paydays . . . closed were the little stores . . . stilled was the tinkling ice-cream bell . . . and as they say in southern Illinois, we had "made do."

EPILOGUE

On a recent trip back to Illinois, I purposefully stopped in Marion so my son and grandson could see the neighborhood where I lived some while I was growing up. We drove down East DeYoung Street past where Mr. Swan had his store, now an empty lot, then up North Glendale Street. Marion was a beautiful place to grow up, to be a boy, with its homecentered atmosphere. While you're busy raising your own family, you think little of your boyhood. But, in later years, your mind goes back. You relive it, and it means so much to you.

—A letter to the author from Charles B. Garrigus, poet laureate of California, Selma, California.

As best I can determine, I was the first person in our extended family, either on my mother's or father's side, to graduate from college. At least, I was one of the first.

I came from a background of farmers and coal miners. Yet I often heard Dad say, "I don't want any of my boys to go below." He was thinking of the dangers, the low pay, and the on-again, off-again working patterns of the mines in the thirties. Conditions are different today and mining is a more attractive vocation. Working conditions are safer, and the pay is much better.

My earliest dreams of college date back, strange as it seems, to a family-owned bus service in Marion. It was operated by the Courtney Moving and Storage Company, located next to Norman's Store on East DeYoung, the one where I bought nickel chunks of ice. I passed there frequently.

Courtney's owned two or three buses that, as I remember, operated chiefly as charters. That was before the day of many school buses in southern Illinois. So for special trips, such as sporting events and band contests, the schools often chartered a Courtney bus for out-of-town trips.

During the thirties, a Courtney bus made a round trip each day to what was then Southern Illinois Normal University in nearby Carbondale, seventeen miles west of Marion. As a boy, I watched this bus manuever its way around town, picking up college students on street corners, here and there. The driver, maybe a student himself, stayed in Carbondale all day and parked the bus near the campus. Riders often sat in the bus during the noon hour, eating their sack lunches or studying. In the afternoon, the bus returned to Marion, dropping off students near their homes.

My earliest and faintest dreams of going to college are associated with this bus. As I watched students getting on and off, it reassured me that there were opportunities for college, if one looked for them.

Each spring, from 1935 to 1938, I rode one of those buses to Carbondale for a district band contest. These contests were held on the campus of the University. I remember the thrill of marching out on the stage of Shryock Auditorium with other band members, then playing our "contest" numbers, directed by George Ashley.

One of my lifelong friends in Marion, Phillip B. Harris, also a graduate of Southern Illinois University, remembers one of those Courtney bus rides even more keenly. As a grade-school boy, Phil was bussed to Carbondale to hear the U.S. Marine Band, directed by John Philip Sousa.

"The concert was in Shryock Auditorium," Phil told me, "and I was so impressed that I can still tell you where I sat. It was in the third row from the front, on the south side. My seat was the fourth from the aisle.

"Today, whenever I hear 'The Stars and Stripes Forever,' a chill runs up my spine as I remember that seat, and that bus trip, and that band playing one of Sousa's best-known marches."

When I was in high school, I spent an afternoon with another friend from Marion, Eugene Vickery, already a student in Carbondale. A few years older than me, Gene was living in a cramped, basement apartment, doing his own cooking. He told me I could attend college, too, if I wanted to.

I'll always be indebted to Southern Illinois University for opening to me the door for a college education. It was close to my home, economical, and the staff and faculty made me welcome. The buildings themselves—on a tiny, postage-stamp-size campus back then—seemed to say, "We're glad to see you; this is your school; you'll like it here; you can make good."

This may seem sentimental and self-serving to today's generation when enrollments are counted in the thousands, not hundreds. But this is how I felt, and I wanted to say it.

It was here I met my future wife, Bessie Emling of Pinckneyville. And it was at the foot of the north steps of Old Main where I asked her for our first date. She said yes and the following week, on a rainy February night, I took her to a ballet—you guessed it—in Shryock Auditorium!

Two of our children graduated from Southern Illinois University. Nancy received her degree in art, and Tim in journalism. Another daughter, Ruth, did some of her college work in the drama department there.

I am also indebted to the University for publishing two of my books about my boyhood in Marion. When I was standing in line at the Marion City Dairy, as a Depression kid, waiting for my nickel's worth of skim milk, or at Swan's Store, wondering what in the world had happened to my penny's worth of minced ham, Carbondale seemed a world away.

But it wasn't and it isn't. For we live in one world, a world made safer and better by education.

Appendix: Grocery Stores in Marion, Illinois, 1939

The following list of all fifty-nine grocery stores in business in Marion in 1939 is printed to illustrate how common they were in the thirties. The information is from the 1939 edition of the Marion City Directory, which also shows the population of "Greater Marion" as 9,575 persons.

To readers outside the Marion area, the list may have little significance. Even so, you may find pleasure in reading the names, much as you would those on an old Civil War monument. It's what these names represent—more than who they were—that gives them meaning. For all across America, in thousands of small towns, there existed such stores as these. And the stories buried in their gas pumps, old ledger books, lard stands, and glass candy cases are probably much like mine.

Arthur Absher, 910 N. Parks
A & P Food Store, 110
  N. Market
A. M. Allen, 716 S. Liberty
J. W. Beasley, 800 S. Holland
J. H. Bradley, 107 E. Union
Buckner's Grocery, 1003
  N. Court
S. S. Burns, 100 S. Champ
Thomas Chaney, 1412 Walnut
J. N. Cooksey, 1801 W. Main
R. L. Cox, 617 W. Main
Charles Crisp, 211 N. Market
Davis Grocery, 1005 E. Main
Dingraudo's Grocery, 704 1/2
  W. White
W. I. Dodd, 614 E. Main
Downtown Market, 109
  W. Main
Duncan's Food Market, 1000
  N. Court
Ira Duryea, 810 N. McLaren
Everybody's Grocery, 509
  E. Boulevard `
Fair St. Market, 104 N. Fair
Feurer Brothers, 113
  S. Russell
George Feurer, 703 W. White
Flucks Market, 412
  N. Market
Garrison Store, 301
  E. Boulevard
Harris Grocery, 800 S. Liberty
W. O. Hartwell, 300
  E. Boulevard
J. E. Hawkins, 1000
  E. McKinley
Paul Haynes, 906
  W. Chestnut
N. S. Hestand, 804 Prairie
W. R. Hodge, 908 S. Court
Ben Hoy, 900 W. Boulevard
Jacks Meats & Groceries, 306
  N. Market
James Clover Farm Store, 404
  S. Court
Kroger Store #2, 400
  N. Market

Kroger Store #28, 707
  W. Main
L. O. Lee, 1209 Walnut
Madison St. Market, 601
  S. Madison
Malden Court Grocery, 900
  S. Court
Mays Home Grocery, 904
  S. Buchanan
George Moseley, 1003
  N. VanBuren
Naborhood Market, 305
  E. Warder
C. E. Nichols, 1015 W. Main
Normans Grocery, 100
  E. DeYoung
Odums Clover Farm Store,
  1100 N. State
Sanders Cash Grocery, 609
  E. Main
Sanders Market, 611
  N. Market
Shoemakers Grocery, 203
  E. Boyton
Simpson's Grocery, 904
  W. White
Smith & Hepler Store, 216
  N. Market
J. C. Swan, 105 E. DeYoung
Swinneys Grocery, 303
  W. Main
Turnage Feed Co., 104
  N. Franklin
V. E. Turner, 504
  E. Boulevard
W. R. Turner, 1003
  E. Boulevard
Vinsons Grocery, 1409
  W. Chestnut
F. M. Walker, 303 E. DeYoung
Wanless Grocery, 611
  N. Court
Waters Store, 213 S. Court
W. T. Watkins, East Main
J. G. Wolland, 920 E. Main